T0113324

THE KNOT AT THE END OF YOUR ROPE

The Knot at the End of Your Rope

Teresa Bell Kindred

HAROLD
SHAW
PUBLISHERS

Wheaton, Illinois

"Signs and Symptoms of Stress" in chapter 10 is reprinted from *Mayo Clinic Guide to Self-Care* with permission of Mayo Foundation for Medical Education and Research, Rochester, MN 55905.

"A Little Effort—A Big Reward" by Brother Lawrence from *Near to the Heart of God: Daily Readings from the Spiritual Classics*, compiled and prepared for the modern reader by Bernard Bangley. Copyright © 1998 by Bernard Bangley. Used by permission of Harold Shaw Publishers.

All Scripture quotations, unless otherwise indicated, are taken from *The Living Bible* © 1971. Used by permission of Tyndale House Publishers, Inc., Wheaton IL 60189. All rights reserved.

Scripture quotations marked THE MESSAGE are from *The Message*. Copyright © 1993, 1994, 1995 by Eugene H. Peterson. Used by permission of NavPress Publishing Group.

Scripture quotations marked NKJV are from the New King James Version. Copyright © 1979, 1980, 1982, Thomas Nelson Inc., Publishers.

Scripture quotations marked NIV are from the HOLY BIBLE, NEW INTERNATIONAL VERSION ®. NIV ®. Copyright 1973, 1978, 1984 by International Bible Society. Used by permission of Zondervan Publishing House. All rights reserved.

The "NIV" and "New International Version" trademarks are registered in the United States Patent and Trademark Office by International Bible Society. Use of either trademark requires permission of International Bible Society.

Scripture quotations marked NLT are taken from the *Holy Bible*, New Living Translation, copyright © 1996. Used by permission of Tyndale House Publishers, Inc., Wheaton, Illinois 60189. All rights reserved.

ISBN-13: 978-0-87788-457-6

Cover illustration by Mary Chambers
Cover design by Thomas Leo and David LaPlaca

Library of Congress Cataloging-in-Publication Data

Kindred, Teresa B.
    The knot at the end of your rope : ten ways to hold on when you are stressed out / by Teresa Bell Kindred.
      p. cm.
    ISBN 978-0-877-88457-6(.)
     1. Stress (Psychology) 2. Stress (Psychology—Religious aspects—Christianity. 3. Stress management. 4. Women—Psychology. I. Title.
BF575.S75K56 1999
155.9'042'082—dc21   99-13080
                                                CIP

146502721

For my mother and father with gratitude
for their legacy of love,
and for my grandmother, Nettie Lee DeMumbrum,
one of the kindest and most forgiving women
God ever made.

Contents

Acknowledgments

Grateful acknowledgment is made to the following people:

My aunts, Mary Alice, Roberta, and Kate, who are my mentors, advisers, and friends.

My cousins (especially Martha and Sarah) for always being there when I need them.

My sister-in-law, Kelly, for her love, laughter, friendship, and high-voltage energy.

My brother, Robert, and nephews, Thomas, Price, and Jackson, for bringing so much joy into my life.

My high school English teachers, Carol and Susan, who have always encouraged me to write and have helped me tremendously.

My church family, for surrounding me with love.

My friends, Annette, Mosier, Pam, Edith, Dorothy, Pam, Sharon, and Kim, for always believing in me.

My editors, Joan Guest and Lil Copan, for their wisdom and knowledge.

My agent, Joyce Farrell, for her expertise.

And to all the women I interviewed, and to those who wrote to me, filled out questionnaires, and emailed their stories to me. I sincerely appreciate your time and the coping strategies you so willingly shared.

Finally, a very special thank-you to my loving and very understanding husband, Bill, and my five precious children: Nick, Rachel, Justin, Grant, and Russell—you make my life complete.

Introduction

Have you ever walked on a treadmill that was going too fast? Your heart pounds as you walk faster and faster in an effort to keep up. Should you adjust the speed? Keep going? Or just give up and get off?

Sometimes our lives become like an out-of-control treadmill. We run from one event to the next until our days become an endless blur of activity. At night we fall into bed exhausted, wondering how we will ever find the energy to get up and do it all over again tomorrow.

Society (particularly the media) tries to convince women that we should look like Ally McBeal, work forty or more hours a week, raise children that are as polite as Wally and Beaver Cleaver, keep our homes clean enough to earn the Good Housekeeping Seal of Approval, and still have enough energy left at the end of the day to slip into something slinky and be ready for romance.

In addition to this, many women feel compelled to volunteer their time for charitable organizations, teach Sunday School class, visit those who are sick, and attend every event their children ever participate in. We fool ourselves into thinking if we can just hang on a little longer, or run a little faster, we can get it all done. Like the pink bunny in the battery commercial, we keep going and going, even when it means neglecting our health and our own personal well-being. When that happens God and our families don't get the best of us . . . they get what is left of us.

How do I know? Because my life became a treadmill and I ran faster and faster—until I almost fell off. Oh, I never came close to looking like Ally McBeal, and the only prize my house ever could have won was the health department's Most Likely To Be Condemned award. I worked forty or more hours a week, fed my family from boxes or bags I picked up at drive-through restaurants, and then fell asleep at night before I could finish reading a bedtime story to my children.

On Sunday mornings I got up an hour early to type the church bulletin. When I finished that job, I turned on the tape player and with the "Theme from Rocky" blaring in the background, I raced up and down the stairs like a madwoman, toting and fetching and matching clothes for everyone. I fed my children a nutritious breakfast of chocolate cocoa puffs or powdered donuts (depending on which box I grabbed first). And usually the twins managed to have dirty diapers right before we walked out the door, so I had to be ready for quick changes (I was the fastest two-diaper changer in the county).

I remember one Sunday morning during church service, I opened my eyes just a tad during prayer to sneak a peek at the children. One of the twins had on unmatched socks and two left shoes. His brother was wearing the two right ones. On down the pew, another son had a liberal dusting of powdered sugar on top of a grape juice mustache. His glasses were on sideways and his hair hadn't been brushed. And another son and our daughter were pinching each other, ready to get into a full-scale battle. My eyes met my husband's and he smiled. I thought he was smiling about the grape juice mustache, or the shoes on the wrong feet. He wasn't.

"Honey," he whispered, "did you know your dress is on backwards and you have an electric roller on top of your head?"

Sunday mornings had become no different than the rest of the week for me. I operated like a loco-motive, full steam ahead. I didn't have time to stop and smell the roses. If there were any flowers in my path, I simply drove over them. I was way be-yond stressed, into a phase I now call *dis-stressed*.

One of my favorite passages in the Bible is Isaiah 40:31: "But they that wait upon the Lord shall renew their strength. They shall mount up with wings like eagles; they shall run and not be weary; they shall walk and not faint."

I told my husband that I wanted to "mount up with wings like eagles" and to "run and not be weary."

He suggested vitamins, so I bought a case of them, but they didn't do anything except increase my appetite. I gained five pounds and began to feel stressed about that too.

I kept running faster and faster, still determined to hang on. I stayed on the treadmill until my health was in jeopardy. My kids were living on pizza and hot-dogs, my house was a disaster area, and the only way I was communicating with my husband was by refrigerator mail.

Then one morning as I was on my way to the school where I taught, I glanced up at the tractor-trailer truck I was passing. In big bold letters written across the side was the word *CASKETS*. I think it was God's way of reminding me that I was going to slow down, one way or the other.

Is this really the way I want to spend my life? I wondered. I pulled off the parkway and did what I usually do when confronted with a crisis: I cried. Not just little dainty-sounding sniffles, but big old gut-wrenching, snot-blowing sobs.

I made it to work that day, but I cried all weekend and convinced myself I was a failure. After all, the other women I saw at church and at work appeared to be okay. If they were handling the stress, then why couldn't I? Didn't Jesus say, "With God, everything is possible" (Matthew 19:26)?

Not every woman lets the stress in her life build until she is as *dis-tressed* as I was, but every woman deals with stress. With God's help I learned how to adjust the speed of my life. You can too.

In this book you will find ten proven strategies to help you hold on to your rope. Some of these suggestions are my own and others were shared with me by women I interviewed while researching this book. Their stories will encourage you, while at the same time reminding you that you are not alone.

May God bless you and may you always remember that the one who holds the universe in the palm of his hand is also the one holding the other end of your rope.

Slow me down, Lord! Ease the pounding of my heart by the quieting of my mind. Steady my hurried pace with a vision of the eternal reach of time. Give me, amidst the confusion of my day, the calmness of the everlasting hills. Break the tensions of my nerves and muscles with the soothing music of singing streams that live in my memory. Teach me the art of taking minute vacations . . . of slowing down to look at a flower, to chat with a friend, to pat a dog, to read a few lines from a good book. Remind me each day of the fable of the hare and the tortoise, that I may know that the race is not always to the swift; that there is more to life than measuring its speed. Let me look upward into the branches of the towering oak and know that it grew great and strong because it grew slowly and well. Slow me down, Lord, and inspire me to send my roots deep into the soil of life's enduring values that I may grow toward the stars of my greater destiny.

Author Unknown

Laugh More, Frown Less

The most wasted of all days is one without laughter.

e. e. cummings

Laughter gives us distance. It allows us to step back from an event, deal with it and then move on.

Bob Newhart

There is a right time for everything: . . . A time to cry; A time to laugh.

Ecclesiastes 3:1, 4

I think bras were invented by a man who didn't like women and wanted to find a subtle method of torturing them. I've never worn one that didn't either cut into me, ride up, or generally make me miserable. Not long ago I came home from work and was outside in the driveway playing with the children when I decided the bra had to go. I unhooked it, reached through the sleeve of my tee-shirt and pulled it through. Then I placed it on the bumper of the van and forgot about it.

Later that afternoon my daughter and I went to the store. When the young man who carried out our groceries spotted my white bra dangling from the rear bumper, he didn't know what to do.

"Well, now," I said with a laugh, "how do you suppose that got there?" I picked up my bra, stuffed it in my purse and opened the door for him. He didn't ask any questions and I didn't volunteer any information. I laughed all the way home. I still laugh whenever I think about the expression on that young man's face.

Laughter is a gift from God and can defuse many stress-bombs if we let it. Well-known actor/comedian Bill Cosby says, "If we can laugh about it, we can survive it." He's right. Not only are people who laugh less stressed, they are also healthier.

In 1964 Norman Cousins, the famous writer, developed a debilitating form of arthritis. Victims of that particular form of arthritis suffer chronic pain and their ability to move freely is often severely limited. In addition to the prescribed traditional therapies, Cousins decided to try something a little different—humor. He watched slapstick comedy, told jokes, and read funny books. Cousins claimed that his "laughter therapy" made his illness less painful, and in 1976 he published an article in the *New England Journal of Medicine* about his experience.

Laughter therapy is nothing new. Thousands of years ago Solomon believed that laughter was good for our health. "A cheerful heart does good like medicine, but a broken spirit makes one sick"

(Proverbs 17:22), he wrote. If we know it is good for us, then why don't we laugh more often? Usually it is because we take life too seriously, as I did one Christmas Eve.

We were on our way to my brother Robert's house for dinner. My older children had packages stacked high in their laps, and one of the younger boys had graciously volunteered to carry the strawberry Jell-O salad for me. We were dressed in our Christmas finery and singing Christmas carols at the top of our lungs when a deer stepped into the path of our van.

My husband was driving, and when he slammed on the brakes, the strawberry Jell-O salad with the whipped cream cheese topping suddenly became airborne. After we were completely stopped, I plucked a strawberry out of my hair and looked behind me to see if everyone had survived.

My son wiped some whipped topping off his glasses, surveyed the mess, and with a child's youthful optimism proclaimed, "Wow, Mom, we all look like someone barfed up a strawberry milkshake on us!"

I didn't see anything funny about my salad being destroyed or about arriving for dinner wearing pink barf on top of my black velvet and lace, but I should have. Laughter would have eased a tense moment and relieved some of the stress I experienced. Besides, the salad didn't go to waste; Robert's coon dogs enjoyed licking it off us!

Evidently the Redbone breed of dog has a sweet tooth, because not long after the salad episode, my sister-in-law Kelly left a case of Sarah Lee chocolate cakes on her back porch (it was winter time and her freezer was full), and her dog, Cool Dude, ate all twelve cakes. Kelly knows how to laugh off tense moments much better than I do. She took one look at the empty boxes and the swollen stomach of the dog and said, "Well, I guess it's true. Nobody doesn't like Sarah Lee!"

We *need* to laugh. But in order to do that, we first have to *perceive* something as funny, and then we have to relax enough to respond appropriately. It's hard to laugh if your face is in a perpetual scowl, or when you're too deeply immersed in your problems.

We attend a small church in a rural area. It is rare for us to have visitors, so when someone new walks through the door, they get the benefit of everyone's undivided attention. One Sunday night Miss Bessie's cousin, Viola, came to visit. It was obvious that she took great pains with her appearance. Her silver gray hair was fluffed to perfection and she wore a flowery cotton dress with a starched lace collar and the highest spiked heels I'd ever seen.

In the back of our church next door to the bathrooms is the baptistery. Right after the service, Miss Viola excused herself to go to the lady's room. From the back of the building we heard a scream, a splash, then silence. Someone had given her the wrong directions and instead of opening the door on the left, she had plunged into the four-foot pool! Luckily, the only thing she injured was her pride. Her beautifully styled hair now looked like wet cat fur and her cotton print dress was limp and glued to her thin little body like a second skin. Once Miss Bessie was sure her cousin wasn't hurt, she burst out laughing, but Miss Viola never cracked a smile.

I didn't laugh about the strawberry salad because I had invested too much time and energy making it. Miss Viola didn't laugh about falling into the baptistery because she was too embarrassed. Sometimes we get so wrapped up in the serious business of living that we forget to relax and enjoy it, and that is especially true when we are attending an event or going to a place, like church, where we are expected to behave in a certain manner.

After our twins came along, getting all five children to church on Sunday mornings made me so tense that by the time I got there, my nerves were stretched tighter than a barbed wire fence. Even when something funny happened (and with five children it almost always does), I often fought the urge to laugh because I had been taught that laughter in church was inappropriate.

In a class that she taught off and on for twenty years, Dr. Annette Goodheart, author of *Laughter Therapy: How to Laugh About Everything in Your Life That Isn't Really Funny,* talked about this desire we have to squelch laughter. According to Dr. Goodheart, "We have cultural myths about laughter that are designed to specifically control [laughter]. There are a lot of places it isn't okay to laugh, and places that it's okay to laugh just a little bit: like at school, the judicial system, religious services, almost all our institutions."

We *should* have a reverent attitude at church, but sometimes things happen making it impossible not to laugh, especially when you have small children. When our twin boys were toddlers, they loved to sit with the preacher's wife at church because she kept her purse well-stocked with gummy bears, crackers, and raisins. One Sunday morning in the middle of the sermon, my angelic son accidentally dropped some of his raisins down the front of this friend's dress; immediately he tried to retrieve them, causing the poor woman to jump around like frog legs in a frying pan. The more she jumped, the more determined my son was to find his raisins. That was one of those occasions when no matter how hard I tried not to, I had to laugh.

During another Sunday morning service, I was trying to get our five-year-old to stop crawling around on the floor, so I grabbed him and sat him down firmly on the pew beside me. He looked at me defiantly, folded his arms, and put on his best pouting face. I decided to ignore him and bowed my head and closed my eyes for prayer.

"Well, Mommy," he said loudly, "the next time you're in the bathroom and you need me to get you toilet paper, you can just forget it!" Laughter allows us to survive embarrassing moments, even when those moments occur during worship.

About the only person my children never managed to distract at church was my great-aunt Lizzie. Of course, she was in her nineties, almost totally deaf, and her eyesight was failing. I once overheard someone ask her why she bothered coming to church at all when she couldn't hear the sermon, sing the songs, or even see the preacher.

"I come to let people know whose side I'm on," she said firmly.

It takes effort to get up on Sunday mornings, get the children up, fed, dressed and to church on time, and depending upon your circumstances, it may cause you a certain amount of stress. If your children are very young, you may even wonder if they get anything out of the service except gummy worms, raisins, and crackers; but they do. Your presence tells them whose side you are on.

Laughter is God's medicine for the soul. It has no adverse side effects, it's not addictive, it's free, you don't need a doctor to prescribe it, and it doesn't come with one of those aggravating child-proof caps! Even people who are critically ill can benefit from a spoonful of laughter.

When my mother was in the final stages of her cancer, she was almost totally incapacitated. Simply moving from her bed to a chair was a major event. One day the family doctor dropped by unexpectedly to check on her. Even in our small town, a doctor making a house call is unheard of.

After he left I went back to her room. She was still sitting in her chair and her eyes were closed, her hands folded together in her lap. I didn't think she knew I was in the room, but she did.

"Two," she whispered and held up the appropriate number of fingers.

"Two what, Mama? Two pills? Two pillows? What is it you need?" I asked.

She shook her head no. It was painful for her even to speak.

"Two hundred dollars. I'll bet he charged me two hundred dollars for that visit," she whispered. Then she grinned.

She had lost weight, lost part of her hair, and lost her ability to walk more than a few steps, but she hadn't lost her sense of humor.

Solomon said, "For the happy heart, life is a continual feast" (Proverbs 15:15, NLT). Is *your* life a continual feast? What aspects of your life can you nourish to make your heart happy?

DEstressors

Identifying Your Stress Points and Developing a Plan of Action

1. What happy things does *your* heart feast on? Can you incorporate those things into your thoughts or activities today?

2. How many times do you laugh during the course of an average day? If you don't laugh at least five times a day, try harder to look at the lighter side of life. Get together with that one friend or that special group of friends who make you smile.

3. Ask yourself if whatever it is that's upsetting you will really matter ten years from now. If the answer is no, then *relax* and respond with laughter!

4. Make a conscious effort to keep a pleasant look on your face. You don't have to smile all the time, but if you "look" happy, chances are you'll feel happier. Plus, you'll get more positive responses from other people.

Kelly's Story

If Laughter Doesn't Work,
Try a Time-Out!

As the mother of three young boys (ages two, five, and eight), I stay extremely busy. My boys are healthy, active children and my husband and I are so very thankful they are, but some days those boys are quite a challenge! I don't know what I'd do if I couldn't laugh about some of the things they get into.

This week they spray-painted our evergreen bushes white. They also flattened my van tires by leaving nails (from one of their many building projects) in the driveway. Then yesterday I looked out the window and the five-year-old was watering his younger brother's wagon—and not with the water hose! You just never know what they'll do next.

Most of the time I'm able to laugh about it, and when I can't, I put them in time-out until I cool off and they have had time to think about what they've done. Time-out is as much for moms as it is for the kids!

Kelly (wife, and mother of three boys)

What Other Women Have to Say

Comments on Breaking the Stress Barrier

I try to laugh out loud at least once a day, email my friends at least twice a week, call my children at least twice a week, and take a good hot bath every night.

Carol (grant writer)

My best stress reliever is my husband, Gary. It's a rare day that he doesn't make me laugh.

Kate (teacher)

I have found that the closer I am to the Lord, the better I feel about myself and the closer I feel to the ones I love. Also, I can't emphasize too much the importance of seeing the funny side of life and being able to laugh at oneself.

Martha (retired teacher)

I like to surround myself with happy people, people who are positive and energetic about life. When you spend too much time around negative people, you tend to become negative, too. When I get stressed it helps if I can find some laughter in the situation. If I can do that, I realize it's not such a stressful time after all.

Julie (stay-at-home mom)

First Things First

First things first, but not necessarily in that
order.

Doctor Who

Decide what you want, decide what you are willing
to exchange for it. Establish your priorities and
go to work.

H. L. Hunt

What's really important in life? Sitting on a
beach? Looking at television eight hours a day? I
think we have to appreciate that we're alive for
only a limited period of time, and we'll spend most
of our lives working. That being the case, I believe
one of the most important priorities is to do
whatever we do as well as we can. We should take
pride in that.

Victor Kiam

Only fools idle away their time.

Proverbs 12:11, NLT

I once heard a preacher tell the story* of a professor who walked into class one day with an empty glass jar. He asked his students to watch what he was about to do closely because when he was finished he was going to ask them a very important question.

First, he placed some large rocks inside the jar until they reached the top. He then asked the students if they thought the jar was full. Most of them answered yes. He reached beneath the table and took a small jar filled with small pebbles, put them in the jar and shook it gently until they sifted down.

"Now is the jar full?" he asked.

His students studied the jar and again most of them answered yes. Again he reached beneath the table, and this time he poured a jar of sand over the rocks until all the crevices were filled.

The students laughed and one said, "Now surely the jar is full."

The professor didn't answer. Instead he reached beneath a table and retrieved another jar, this one filled with water. He took the water and poured it over the rocks, gravel, and sand.

"Now I am finished," the professor said. "What have you learned?"

"That you can cram a lot of junk in a jar," one wise guy cracked.

The professor shook his head sadly. "No, my

---

*Story attributed to writer/speaker Stephen Covey.

friend. The lesson here is that when it comes to life, you have to put your big rocks in first."

Not long ago I was reading a magazine and I ran across a poll that asked the question, "What do you never have enough of?" The number one answer wasn't money; it was time. With all the modern conveniences we have to make our lives easier, why does it seem like we have less time, not more?

Because the same technology that brings us appliances to lighten our work load also provides us with other options for spending our time. While the dishwasher is doing the dishes, and the washer and dryer are taking care of the laundry, we can entertain ourselves with television or by surfing the Internet—things our great-grandmothers could not have imagined. And while these things are not bad, they can distract us and consume time the way a sponge soaks up water.

To illustrate what I mean, just for a moment imagine that time is money, real dollars and cents: instead of opening up a savings account and reserving some of it, we deposit the whole amount in our checking account and do our best to spend every single dime.

We shouldn't bankrupt ourselves financially or emotionally, but for some of us, saving time (or money!) is not an easy thing to do. My friend Susan is a former "time spendthrift." Her eyes were recently opened to the compounded interest she earned when she found the courage to say no.

Susan was offered a leadership position in her community and for a short time she seriously considered accepting it. Before her children were born she had been active in local civic organizations, but as her life became busier she had withdrawn from community service. Now she yearned to get involved once more. When Susan asked me what I thought, I suggested she make a "priority list." Susan took my words to heart and wrote down all her commitments and then prioritized them. When she looked at the sheet of paper she quickly saw that her list was full and there wasn't anything on it she was willing to give up. Reluctantly, she turned down the offer.

A few weeks later Susan learned that a friend of hers, Barbara, had taken the job. "I can't help it," Susan confided to me. "I'm jealous."

Within just a few months it was obvious that Barbara was doing an outstanding job. Every week the local paper was full of changes and improvements that Barbara had initiated.

A few weeks later Susan and I had dinner together at a local restaurant. "You know," she said over dessert and coffee, "I am so thankful I didn't take that job we discussed. Barbara was the right choice, not me. She's doing a wonderful job and I wrote her a letter and told her so last week."

Susan is clearly a very talented individual as well and I reminded her about her priority list. "If this job had been closer to the top of your list you would have done just as well as Barbara," I said.

She shook her head slowly. "No, I wouldn't. I have three children, a full-time job. I'm the church secretary and I'm helping my sister take care of our grandmother. Barbara has no children and has always had a flair for motivating people. My ego wanted me to think I could handle another responsibility but the truth is I couldn't have. I wouldn't have devoted the time and energy to the job that Barbara has, and then I would have been frustrated because I wasn't giving it my all."

If we want to reduce stress we have to establish our priorities and then put our big rocks in the jar first.

DEstressors

Identifying Your Stress Points and Developing a Plan of Action

1. What are the big rocks in your life? In other words, what is most important to you? Are you putting too many big rocks in the jar first? If not, are you cramming them into whatever space is left? Identify two of your "pebbles"—less important activities. Can you get rid of them so you can fit in those important rocks?

2. Make a list of the ten things that matter most to you. The next time you're in doubt as to whether or not to do something, ask yourself, "Is this directly connected to those ten things on my priority list?" If it isn't, let it go.

3. Proverbs 12:15 says, "Fools think they need no advice, but the wise listen to others" (NLT). Discuss your priorities with someone whose opinion you value. Ask that person's opinion on how many rocks you should put in your jar. Take that advice into consideration before making any major changes in your lifestyle.

Sarah's Story

Rediscovering My Dreams

I can't remember a time in my life when I didn't want a college degree. But I had to put my dreams on the back burner for several years while my children were young. At that time we only had one car, which meant I couldn't get out much. And all the other moms I knew worked outside their home. I found staying at home with two small children to be very stressful. One day while we were watching *Sesame Street,* an all-animal orchestra performed. All these different barnyard animals began barking, mooing, oinking, etc., to a piece of classical music. My nerves were so shot, I almost lost it. I guess that was the first time I realized that I was not meant to be a permanent stay-at-home mom.

I was almost thirty years old when I went back to college. In a way going back to school relieved some of my stress, but it also brought on mountains of other problems. For one thing, I felt guilty for spending so much time on myself.

One of the main things that kept me going was the inspiration of an aunt that I was especially close to. She had gone back to school when her children started school, and she was a firm believer that everyone should have a college education. Even though she had died years before I returned to school, I could hear her in the back of my mind saying, "You can do it. You can be anything you want to be."

While I was taking classes I did my best to keep my children my top priority. I purposely planned all my classes (except one, which I couldn't change) so that I could be home by the time they got off the bus.

One way I relieve stress is by allowing myself the luxury of a good cry now and then. Many times I need to sit by myself on my porch swing and just let the tears flow. It always seems to help.

I am doing my student teaching now and next spring I will walk through the graduation line. It feels wonderful to finally have my dream of a college degree come true. I praise God for helping me get this far!

*Sarah (wife, mother of three,
and soon-to-be college graduate)*

What Other Women Have to Say

Comments on Breaking the Stress Barrier

I find stress comes not in one area of my life but in trying to juggle all the parts of the whole. Priorities are often not clear and many things need to be done. If you give up one job, then you stress about another part of life. The best way I've found to deal with stress is through church. We go to keep ourselves centered on what is important in life. Prayer also helps give peace in the midst of the storm. I try my best not to sweat the small stuff.

Geneva (medical technologist)

The current buzz phrase for women (and men) who work outside the home is *home life/work life balance.* Human Resource departments find fancy ways to tell you about how important it is, and managers *say* they put family first . . . but it's all a lot of talk until you as an individual decide what your priorities are and *implement* them. It means asking yourself *important* questions, like, will this matter five years from now? If it won't, don't sweat it. When pushed to add "one more project," push back!

Ask your supervisors what they want you to *not*

do, in order to *do* this! Mark your boundaries. If you, in your mind or—even better—on paper, decide where you will draw the line with your time and energy, you will feel more in control of your life and of the things that are most important to you. Remember, none of us is Superwoman, no matter how much we would like to convince ourselves that we are.

Annette (pharmaceutical sales representative, wife and mother)

The one thing that comes to my mind often and helps me so much is the question: Will it matter to me in ten years? Most of the time the answer is no. If the answer is yes, I dig in for the long haul and pray for the strength to endure.

Kris (stay-at-home mom)

I do a goal worksheet once a year to keep clear on the major priorities and goals in my life. This helps me focus on the things that are my bedrock: my marriage, and my physical and emotional well-being. When I hit that wall—the one where I look at the week's to-do list and admit to myself that no human being could get all that stuff done even given a *month*—then I just slash everything that doesn't have to do with my bedrock goals or with keeping my job. I don't like doing it, but there is comfort in knowing that I can back off and keep only to the things that are in line with where I really want to be in the long run.

Sandy (computer programmer, age 39)

Recognize Your Value

They talk about a woman's sphere as though it
   had a limit.
But, there's not a life, or death, or birth,
Without a woman in it.

C. E. Bowman, adapted

Next to God, we are indebted to women, first for
life itself, and then for making it worth having.

C. Nestell Bovee

Charm can be deceptive and beauty doesn't last,
but a woman who fears and reverences God shall
be greatly praised. Praise her for the many fine
things she does. These good deeds of hers shall
bring her honor and recognition from even the
leaders of the nations.

Proverbs 31:30-31

Not long ago my sister-in-law
and I had to be out of town for a weekend women's
retreat. We took my daughter, Rachel, along with
us and left our boys at home with their fathers. It

was wonderful to get away. We spent an entire weekend without having to watch a single sporting event on television or pick up one dirty sock, but I should have known I would pay for such luxury when I returned home.

When I walked into the house late Sunday night and tripped over three empty pizza boxes and a trash bag full of empty soda cans, it wasn't hard to guess what had taken place. I followed a trail of moon pie wrappers downstairs to the big-screen television and found all my boys (even the big one they call Daddy) piled up on the couch watching a football game. They all looked up at me with a hand-caught-in-the-cookie-jar expression.

I had a sneaking suspicion that no one (except my husband) had brushed his teeth or taken a bath since I had been gone. And I didn't dare ask if the homework was done. By the time I got the last one out of the tub and in the bed, I was exhausted.

As I kissed Justin good-night he looked up at me and said with a wistful sigh, "You know, Mommy, we sure had a good time while you were gone."

I suppose such a statement should be a blow to my ego, but I've learned to think of myself as a V.I.M. (Very Important Mama). I know that when I am not home my boys enjoy their freedom, but someone has to save them from themselves and it might as well be me. Besides, who else loves them enough to unroll their stinking ball-socks?

I know that whether my children act like it or not, I am important to them, and that increases my feeling of self-worth. But how I feel about my-self can't depend solely on others: It has to come from within. No matter what age we are or what stage of life we are in, to have a strong sense of self-esteem is crucial. We *should* feel important—after all, the book of Ephesians calls us the "work-manship" of Jesus Christ and the book of Proverbs tells us we're "more valuable than rubies." Yet, for one reason or another, many women *consistently* don't see themselves as workmanship or as more valuable than rubies. And constant feelings of infe-riority lead to stress.

This kind of stress leads to even more serious problems. When I was teaching, I was aware of stu-dents who lacked self-confidence, and I watched them constantly short-change themselves. Be-cause they didn't believe they could succeed at certain things, often they didn't. And it was usu-ally the girls, not the boys, I noticed, who lacked self-esteem. I saw beautiful young women who thought they were plain, or even ugly. I saw thin girls who felt fat. I saw girls with enough skill and talent to be doctors, lawyers, teachers, or any-thing they chose to be, getting married and having babies not because they wanted to, but because they believed that was the only option available to them. Lack of self-confidence wasn't the only ob-stacle many of these girls faced, but it was one of the biggest hurdles in their path. Many of them couldn't get over it, no matter how hard I tried to encourage them to respect themselves and their abilities.

Because I observed so many girls struggling with this problem, I became determined to create a strong sense of worth in my own daughter, Rachel, as she was nearing her teen years. I encourage her now as well to believe in herself and her abilities. I frequently tell Rachel (and her brothers) that they have the resources to achieve great things in life if they apply themselves. But merely *being told* about the importance of self-worth isn't enough.

Another way to increase our sense of self-worth is to choose female role models who are self-confident—the more positive role models, the better—and role models aren't just for the young. We all need role models. I find that I learn self-confidence best when I surround myself with supportive and self-confident women.

A few years ago my cousin and I initiated an annual weekend retreat for the females in our family. There is only one rule: You have to be at least twelve years old to attend (this allows the mothers of young children the freedom to take a break from their younger children and participate in everything we do). We take turns being "in charge" of the retreat, and every year we go to a different place. We eat together, shop together, go for long walks, play games, and stay up late talking. It's a wonderful opportunity to bond, and it lets our daughters see a side of us that they wouldn't normally see. After just one weekend with these self-confident women, I come home energized and feeling important—important enough that I could shrug off my son's comments about how much fun he and his brothers have without me.

Self-worth isn't determined by where we live, our occupation, or the size of our bank account. It is determined by believing with all our hearts that God made us special and that our God-given talents can and should be used—until we are the best that we can be.

DEstressors

Identifying Your Stress Points and Developing a Plan of Action

1. Think of a woman you consider self-confident. What makes her that way? List the ways her attitude has a positive impact on her life.

2. In what areas of your life do you have the least confidence (work, home, school, children)? Discuss this lack of confidence with a woman you feel *is* confident in those areas you feel weak. Ask her for suggestions.

3. Recognize that you are Christ's workmanship and treat yourself with respect! Stop telling yourself you don't deserve that good job or that place on the church committee or that higher degree. You *do* deserve those things— as challenging as they may be. If God gave you the gifts for a task, go for it!

Gay's Story

How Prayer Helped Me Climb My Mountain

When I was only a junior in high school, I fell in love and got engaged. My friends and family begged me to attend college—I was the valedictorian of my class—but I was young, in love, and determined to get married. So I applied at a local bank and started working as a cashier soon after I graduated.

My husband joined the army and within a year our first son was born. Eighteen months later a second son followed. While I stayed home with the children, my husband was sent on tour. He was gone for eighteen months. The boys and I counted the days until his return. We had a calendar and we marked off each day until "Daddy" would be home.

My husband had been home only one week before I learned he'd been living with another woman while overseas. I was devastated, and I couldn't save my marriage. We soon divorced. At that time I was only twenty-three years old and my sons were just three and four.

Women didn't make as much money back then, and I had to work two jobs to make ends meet. I worked at a bank during the day and sold Tupperware at night. I wasn't a pushy sales lady and as a result I was only semi-successful with my Tupperware sales. But every time I had a financial crisis in my life, someone would call and ask for me to do a party for them. I know that wasn't accidental: It was God's way of helping me.

My mother kept my children while I worked, and it was a relief to know they were well cared for. Yet, they still suffered because of the divorce. I would come home at night exhausted and not have the patience with them I should have had. Everyone who knew me thought I was handling things well, but it was all a front. At night I would try and hold together long enough to get the children in bed. Then I would fall apart. My ex-husband was giving me financial support, but I had no emotional support . . . until I turned to God.

Those years were really tough. Divorce is common today but back then my children were the only ones in their classroom with divorced parents. I was also the first person in my family to get divorced, and that was stressful. I was the only mom at the barber shop, basketball games, and practices: places that fathers usually took their kids.

It took about four years after my divorce before I learned to be content and to stop questioning "Why me?" That's when things finally started getting better.

When I think back on those years and how hard they were, one event stands out in my mind. It was winter and I wasn't accustomed to driving on snow and ice. Every morning I had to take the boys to my mother's house before I went to work. The roads were treacherous. There was one hill between my house and my mother's that even experienced drivers had trouble climbing in the snow. I knew it was going to be difficult for me to make it to the top. I had the boys buckled up in the back seat because I knew I would have to make a running shoot from the bottom of the hill. Three or four times I tried, but I just couldn't make it. I started praying that God would help me climb the hill. I didn't realize it at the time, but I was praying out loud. I backed the car up and tried one last time. The strangest thing happened. It was almost like someone lifted my car and carried us to the top of the hill! I sat there for a moment and then I burst out crying.

One of my boys saw my tears and said, "But Mommy, why are you crying now? God got us up the hill!"

That event served as a reminder that if I would only ask for his help, he would carry me.

Gay (secretary, age 46)

What Other Women Have to Say

Comments on Breaking the Stress Barrier

Recently I have been going through some tough times. My basement has been flooded for eleven weeks, I'm unemployed, and I've been diagnosed with fibromyalgia. I live in a small community and have not made many friends here. My church family is thirty miles away.

To keep my mind off my problems I get a cup of coffee or hot tea and sit on my patio. There I listen to the birds and take stock of those things I have to be thankful for. When dealing with stress it helps me to remember what my mom has always so fondly stated: "This too shall pass."

Melanie (licensed practical nurse)

One of my personal hang-ups is that I absolutely hate being late. When I realized how much being late upset me, I decided to do something about it. I took a stress management class. Of course, I was always the first one to arrive. When the teacher found out about my problem, she made me stand outside the door until everyone else was in the classroom—and sometimes even longer. I finally realized that the world wasn't going to end if I was late.

Now, if my problems are something that I feel I can't handle I take a deep breath and think of the worst-case scenario. I tell myself that even if I am late for work, I am still alive and in good health and being late won't change that.

Diane (registered nurse)

Treat Your Body Like a Temple, Not a Condemned Building

Exercise alone provides psychological and physical benefits. However, if you also adopt a strategy that engages your mind while you exercise, you can get a whole host of psychological benefits fairly quickly.

James Rippe, M.D.

To resist the rigidity of old age one must combine the body, the mind and the heart—and to keep them in parallel vigor one must exercise, study, and love.

Karl von Bonstetten

A bear, however hard he tries, grows tubby without exercise.

Author unknown, inspired by A. A. Milne's Pooh books

Didn't you realize that your body is a sacred place, the temple of the Holy Spirit? Don't you see that you can't live however you please, squandering what God paid such a high price for? The physical part of you is not some piece of property belonging to the spiritual part of you. God owns the whole works.

1 Corinthians 6:19, THE MESSAGE

Have you ever tried to function on four or five hours of sleep, eaten fast-food meals in between appointments, then collapsed on the couch at night in a state of total exhaustion? Does your weekly aerobics class consist of opening the lids of hamburger boxes and twisting off soft-drink tops?

How can we take care of our families or meet our obligations at work when we refuse to take care of ourselves?

Too much stress, or stress that is poorly managed, can and will affect your physical well-being. Forty-four percent of all adults suffer some adverse health effects from stress. Seventy-five to ninety percent of all doctor's visits are for stress-related ailments and complaints. And stress is often linked to the six leading causes of death: heart disease, cancer, lung ailments, accidents, cirrhosis of the liver, and depression leading to suicide.

Now the good news: There is something you can do about stress.

Every spring we are motivated when we see ourselves for the first time in last year's bathing suit.

"This year I'm going to firm up that flab!" we say, but our good intentions vanish faster than the smoke from the barbecue grill. Before we know it it's time for the bathing suit to go back in the drawer until the next spring. After so many years of doing this we begin to think that enough is enough and wonder if there isn't an easier way to look better. We take our dollars and visit clinics and parlors where we can have our tummies tucked, skin peeled, fat liposuctioned, hair colored, and wrinkles removed. But the truth is, if we would treat our bodies like temples instead of condemned buildings, we wouldn't have to spend so much time and money on maintenance.

Remember what your mother used to tell you about eating right, getting enough sleep, exercising, and wearing sun screen? Once again your mother was right.

"Okay," you respond, like a true skeptic: "I can leave off the french fries, rub on some sun screen, and I don't mind taking a nap now and then, but *exercise?*"

I understand that lack of enthusiasm. For years I felt that way too. *Any kind of exercise is about as pleasant as a big dose of caster oil,* I thought. But during one incredible period of stress, I changed my mind.

When my mother was diagnosed with colon cancer, my life was turned upside down. At that point, we only had three children: the oldest was eight, our daughter was five, and the baby was just three. My husband, Bill, was working at night and going to school during the day to finish his master's degree, and his father had just been diagnosed with terminal cancer too.

Within the space of just a few months, my world shrank to the confines of my mother's house. My life began to revolve around other people's needs, and there simply wasn't enough of me to go around. That's when I started walking.

At first it was just a way to get out of the house, but I soon realized that it not only helped with the stress, it gave me a quiet place to think, to meditate, and more importantly, to pray. There have been periods of time in my life since then, when for one reason or another I've stopped walking for a couple of weeks, but most days I walk two to four miles.

Sometimes I go with a friend. Sometimes it's just me and God. The more stressed I am, the more I walk; and the more I walk, the better I feel.

Exercise has its benefits. I remember once my son Justin ran up behind me. He was only about five years old then and not very tall. When he ran into me from behind, his hands landed right on my bottom. He gave it a little squeeze and then looked up at me and said, "Wow, Mom, your bottom feels just like biscuit dough!"

You've heard of buns of steel? Well, I had buns of dough. Walking helped that problem, too. But as much as I love walking, there are days when I'm simply not motivated. On those days I remind myself what I felt like before I started exercising and that helps get me going again.

None of us would go to the grocery store, fill up a cart, and then leave without paying. We know that you don't get something for nothing. Yet that's exactly what we do when we wish for good health without exercising, eating right, or getting enough rest. Our bodies are a gift from God (say that to the mirror the next time you try on that swimsuit!) and it's up to us to use them, not abuse them. And besides taking care of them, we need to develop a comfort with our looks at all ages and stages of our lives.

Angela is one of the most beautiful women I know, inside and out. She has gorgeous hair, a cute figure, and a smile that lights up the room, but she has a hang-up about her legs. "I hate my cellulite thighs and varicose veins," she confided to me and another friend one day over lunch.

Janet nodded sympathetically. "I have crows feet three inches deep at the corners of my eyes," she moaned.

Truthfully, I had never noticed Angela's legs or Janet's crows feet, but I understood their worries.

"To cover up my gray hair I've been experimenting with hair color. I either get it too red or too dark. Can you believe this color? I look like a pumpkin," I said as I ran my hands through my hair in frustration.

They looked at each other and laughed. Neither one of them had noticed my hair.

We came away from our lunch convinced that we don't see ourselves the way others see us. How do you see yourself? Have you let television and magazines convince you that only young, thin women can be beautiful? It simply isn't the truth. My grandmother is eighty-six years old, she is neither young nor thin and yet she grows more beautiful with each passing year. Beauty doesn't come in any particular size or color; it comes from the soul and from a person's capacity to love.

And if we love ourselves the way we are commanded to, we will treat our bodies the way we would treat our mother's best china—with tenderness and a fair amount of pride.

DEstressors

Identifying Your Stress Points and Developing a Plan of Action

1. How do you treat your body? What have you done this week that has shown respect for your body as God's temple? What have you done that has treated it like a condemned building?

2. Do you find yourself making excuses for your physical appearance? If so, why? Pick one negative opinion you have about your physical being and name three things you can do to make your attitude more positive.

3. What lifestyle changes can you make that will improve your health?

Easy
Steps to developing a
Healthier Lifestyle*

Eating Habits

🕸 Make a list of everything you eat in a day, every day for two weeks.

🕸 Look for patterns. Do you eat more in the morning or at night? Do you eat less or more when you're stressed? Are the foods you snack on good for you, or are you consuming junk food?

🕸 Find a friend who is knowledgeable about nutrition, someone who is qualified to help you evaluate your eating patterns. (Most of us know someone in the health field—doctor, nurse, dietitian—who would be willing to help us.) Review your list together.

🕸 Write down the list of good suggestions you received and post these helps on your refrigerator door. Encourage yourself to follow those health guidelines by putting a motiva-

---

*Always discuss plans for any radical changes in your eating or exercise habits with your doctor.

tional quote above your list. Perhaps something like Philippians 4:13, "For I can do everything God asks me to with the help of Christ who gives me the strength and power."

Exercise

⊛ Exercise with a friend. You can motivate each other to keep fit.

⊛ Set short-term, attainable goals. Something like: "This week I will exercise three times, for thirty minutes at a time" would work. If thirty minutes is more than you can spare at a stretch, try fifteen minutes in the morning, and fifteen minutes later in the day.

⊛ If your workout schedule isn't working, try to exercise at a different time of the day. If you aren't happy with the way your exercise fits into your schedule, you won't stick with it.

If you haven't found your athletic niche yet,
⊛ make a list of all the sports activities available to you. Choose the three you like the best. Try a different one every day; if none of those suit you, choose three more and try them. Keep going until you find the activity that suits you best.

When it comes to exercising, you've already won half the battle if you find an activity that you enjoy. So, if you don't like aerobics, *don't* enroll in an aerobics class. If you don't like tennis, don't waste your money taking lessons.

Martha's Story

When Our Temples Betray Us: My Experience with Breast Cancer

One of the most stressful times of my life was when I learned I had breast cancer. If a friend came to me now and told me she'd been diagnosed with the same thing, I would tell her to surround herself with support and let people help her. Most women are *givers* and they feel guilty about *receiving* from others. Don't! Your turn to give will come again.

I would also tell my friend that it's important to realize that some people know what to say and do in crisis situations, and others don't.

When I was first diagnosed with cancer, Bethany, a close friend of mine, really let me down. Then when my cancer recurred, she showed up on my doorstep unexpectedly. I invited her in and she told me she had come to see me for two reasons: "The first thing I have to tell you is I'm sorry for being such a lousy friend when you went through this the first time. The second thing I want to say is, this time I will be there for you." And she was. She was at the hospital the morning I went to surgery and other times I needed her.

I was scheduled for my mastectomy at five o'clock

in the morning and I wasn't expecting anyone to be there except my closest family. Was I surprised when they rolled me down the hall and thirty or so people were there to kiss and hug me and to let me know they were praying for me. I appreciated their support so much. Not just for me, but for my parents, my husband, and my children. This has been so hard for them, especially my mother.

After my first diagnosis, I turned to my mother for support. I felt like my husband wasn't able to deal with the chemo and radiation and that my mother could. She went with me to every treatment, and while I deeply appreciated her being there, I resented the fact that my husband wasn't. It caused friction between the two of us. I didn't realize it at the time, but he felt left out because I assumed he didn't want to go with me. When my cancer recurred he said, "This time I'm going with you." It made it so much easier because it wasn't just me fighting cancer, it was the two of us fighting it together.

Both times after I was diagnosed, I noticed a definite retreat into myself. I guess you could say I went into a self-preservation mode. I had to take care of my needs first in order to survive. As I began to get well I had to make a conscious effort not to be selfish—to come out of that mode. Sometimes when people face a crisis, they retreat into themselves but they never come out of it. They remain absorbed in their problems and their own lives. I didn't want to do that and I've worked hard not to.

We live in a relatively small town and I've been a teacher in the public schools for twenty-one years, so it's safe to say a lot of people know me and they all know I had a mastectomy. But the funny thing is, instead of being embarrassed about it, I feel honored. I know others are looking to me to see how I react, so I always do my best to give the glory to God for helping me through my crisis.

Martha (teacher, wife, mother of three daughters, volunteer for the American Cancer Society)

What Other Women Have to Say

Comments on Breaking the Stress Barrier

Exercise is the best method for me to deal with stress. The worst tension headache I have can be relieved by thirty minutes of good, strong, sweaty exercise. Not only is it good for you and increases circulation, but it allows you to take a mental time-out.

Leah (lawyer, single)

I find that my physical state has great impact on my stress level. If I'm in top shape, it's easier to have a positive attitude and cope with problems as they occur.

Mary Alice (wife, grandmother, and retired teacher)

I pray, read my Bible for guidance in raising my children and in my life, and I walk or ride my exercise bike almost every day after my girls go to bed.

Laura (system consultant, mother)

Cultivate Patience Instead of Anger

Holding on to anger, resentment and hurt only gives you tense muscles, a headache and a sore jaw from clenching your teeth. Forgiveness gives you back the laughter and the lightness in your life.

Joan Lunden

When angry, count to ten before you speak; if very angry, an hundred.

Thomas Jefferson

Kind words can be short and easy to speak, but their echoes are truly endless.

Mother Teresa

People with good sense restrain their anger; they earn esteem by overlooking wrongs.

Proverbs 19:11, NLT

One morning when I was still teaching at the local high school, I was getting ready for work and running late. My son Russell wasn't helping things any. He was about three years old and three feet tall then, and he had attached himself to my leg like fuzz on Velcro while he whined about my upcoming departure.

"Russell," I said sharply, "I don't like it when you whine."

His bottom lip went out and trembled. Big tears rolled down his cheeks. "Mommy," he said softly, "I don't like it when you yell."

Now I was the one who was three feet tall.

Angry words can do a lot of damage and cause unnecessary stress. At times I've considered carrying a roll of duct tape in my purse so that I can slap a piece over my mouth when I feel the urge to vent my anger verbally, but I know that holding anger in isn't healthy. If yelling or keeping anger inside isn't the answer, what is?

Pat Holt and Grace Ketterman's wonderful book *When You Feel Like Screaming: Help for Frustrated Mothers* has a suggestion that applies to women of all ages: "As one stress hits, deal with it instantly. Dealing with it means accepting the stress—not denying its existence. Find out what you can do about the stress, decide who can help you with it, and set a specific time when you will put the plan into motion. Then put that stress out of your mind."

That's exactly what my friend Annette did when a surprise visit from a relative threatened to send her off the deep end:

As a sales representative in the ever-changing medical field, I am on a pretty steep continual learning curve, and am required to attend tons of training meetings, often to practice sales presentations and take tests. I used to work for weeks prior to the meeting to make sure I knew all my material. One Sunday afternoon I found myself facing a Monday meeting with only the afternoon to prepare. Out of the blue, my husband's uncle, who is a truck driver, called and said he was two miles away and would I please come get him so he could see where we lived. John was out of town, so I loaded up the girls, went to get him and spent the afternoon and evening entertaining our unexpected guest.

Monday morning came and I had to give my presentation as expected—without any preparation. I mean, it was cold turkey all the way!

It turned out that my manager loved the presentation, and out of over two hundred representatives in our whole region, I won an award for the best presentation in my entire division. It taught me to take myself less seriously and to just nail down the basics. When you do that it works just as well, and believe me, it's a lot less stressful!

When life throws you a curve ball, deal with it and move on. Resist the temptation to let anger control your reaction to stress. Don't let anger build a wall between you and someone you love.

Recently while I was waiting for one of my children at an after-school ball practice, a father walked into a gym full of teenagers and yelled loudly for his son to come on, that it was time to go. The tone of his voice made it obvious that he was very angry. All the chaos and noise in the gym suddenly ceased. The teenager's face flushed bright red as he walked across the gym floor. The occasional squeak of his sneakers was the only sound in the auditorium.

"I said, hurry up!" yelled the father. "Next time you can find another ride home from practice. I've got too much to do to be hauling you around."

I cringed. And so did his son. His anger reminded me that words can be a dagger used to inflict wounds that may never heal, or—when they are spoken with *love*—they can be a beautiful gift.

Here are a few steps that I have found helpful when it comes to controlling anger so that my words will be gifts—not daggers. Try them; they may be a good starting place for you. The first step in bridling your tongue is *believing* you can control your temper. There are some people who have convinced themselves that they have no control over anger, and they use this as an excuse to fly off the handle. "Oh you know how I am," they say in their own defense. But when we hurt the people we love with our angry words, it's time to go beyond excuses and take positive steps toward working through our anger issues.

Next, try dealing with your anger by using a

stalling device: something that will delay your response until you've had time to cool off. Many people claim that counting to ten, twenty, or even thirty helps them remember to think before they speak. Others recommend going for a walk or a drive, and I know one woman who locks herself in the bathroom until she knows she won't be hurting anyone with angry, uncontrolled words.

Then, think through what you are going to say before you say it. Once angry words are spoken it is impossible to take them back. You might want to step in front of a mirror. Observe your expression. Do you look calm, or like you're about to explode? Speak your thoughts out loud at that mirror. Are the words you are speaking constructive or destructive? If they are destructive, stall until you are more calm.

Before you speak, keep in mind this proverb, "A gentle answer turns away wrath, but a harsh word stirs up anger" (Proverbs 15:1, NIV).

DEstressors

Identifying Your Stress Points and Developing a Plan of Action

1. Have your words been gifts to the people you've talked to today? Great. Keep going! Make a point of using your words as gifts at least three more times today.

   Have your words been daggers? Then keep in mind that "love covers a multitude of sins" (1 Peter 4:8, NLT) and determine to use word gifts today for the people you may have fired daggers at yesterday.

2. Do you sometimes wonder where your anger comes from? Pray about the issues surrounding your anger. Take the time to think about the sources and to discover possible solutions. While you're thinking about it, try to relieve some of your tension. Maybe make a cup of decaf tea or hot chocolate. Many people find that certain warm beverages soothe them.

3. Soak away your angry tensions (or any tensions, for that matter) in the bath-

tub. Light candles and put on a CD or tape of soothing music while you relax. (Watch out for electrical appliances near the tub that could definitely add stress!)

4. Still have tensions? Treat yourself to a massage—it can often provide emotional and spiritual benefits along with the physical ones.

Jane's Story

The Biggest Test: Discovering the Color of Love

Both my children made the mistake of having children outside of marriage. This has helped me realize that all people make mistakes and that these are the times my children need loving parents the most.

The Bible teaches us that we are not to judge, but until this happened to my children, I had a hard time separating the mistake from the person.

I've also had struggles dealing with my daughter's biracial marriage. It has tested me more than anything else in my life. I fought this until I saw clearly my choices: either reject my child or help her deal with the difficult choice she had made. I've learned and grown greatly because I was forced to accept the fact that appearance means nothing. What matters is *beneath* the color of our skin.

In the last six years I've grown as a person and a Christian because I've dealt with stressful issues that I never dreamed I would have to face. I have learned to pray, and I rely on God to help me.

Sometimes we just float through life until something happens to get our attention. God definitely got my attention and I know I'm a changed person because he did.

Now I know that the love of God, family, and friends will help me through anything. I also do my best to remember to say thank you for all he has blessed me with. If I ever forget how fortunate I am, all I have to do is look at my three beautiful grandchildren and they remind me.

Jane (teacher, wife, mother, grandmother)

What Other Women Have to Say

Comments on Breaking the Stress Barrier

When dealing with stress the first thing I do is count to ten, taking deep breaths to calm myself. Then I pray that God would help me deal with the problem. I also like to walk around the block to clear my head.

Jennifer (preschool teacher)

The best way I deal with stress is to escape for a little while. If nothing else, I go to my bedroom and shut the door. I read, or surf on the Internet. The stress is still there, but it gives me some breathing room to relax and think about how I could deal with the problems that I am facing.

Sarah (wife, mother, college student)

I never realized the importance of Lamaze in all areas of my life. I have found the relaxation techniques I thought were only for childbirth to be vitally important in dealing with my family in difficult situations, in coping with dental procedures, in handling traffic on a hectic day. I counsel all women to take Lamaze regardless of their fertility status.

Lori (age 35, education volunteer and church resource room coordinator)

I am a massage therapist, and I've found that if a therapist has a spiritual connection and is able to use it in his or her work, then the session will be more successful. At the beginning of the session, I always take into account the spiritual, physical, and emotional state of the person seeking relief. Before I begin, I say a prayer for guidance, that I may provide the relief that a client seeks. I feel that my large hands are a gift, and I receive many blessings in my life because of the service I provide.

Kay (wife and massage therapist)

Create a Place of Peace

Be still, and know that I am God.

Psalm 46:10, NIV

I can take my telescope and look millions and millions of miles into space, but I can lay it aside and go into my room, shut the door, get down on my knees in earnest prayer, and see more of heaven, and get closer to God than I can assisted by all the telescopes and material agencies of earth.

Isaac Newton

Do not pray for easy lives. Pray to be stronger people. Do not pray for tasks equal to your powers. Pray for power equal to your tasks. Then the doing of your work will be no miracle, but you will be the miracle.

Phillips Brooks, adapted

Zach, one of our son's best friends, was having dinner with us one night. As usual, everyone was at the table except me. I was running back and forth to the kitchen for first one thing then another, when I happened to overhear Justin ask Zach a question.

"Hey, Zach. Does your mom ever sit down?"

"Nope."

"Mine either." Justin replied. "It must be a mom thing."

The busier we are, the harder it is to sit still. But if we don't find the time to sit still, to reflect, and to pray, it is impossible to have inner peace. And if we don't have inner peace, then we are going to be stressed.

When I was teaching, we occasionally had staff meetings that kept me until supper time. One night after a meeting I came home exhausted. The children were hungry and needed help with their homework. Bill was working late and my nerves were stretched tighter than the maternity jeans I wore before the twins were born. After I had cooked supper and supervised baths and homework, Bill finally arrived home. I practically ran over him trying to get out the door.

It was a little past dusk and the night was warm and clear. A few stars were just beginning to twinkle. I found a dogwood tree in full bloom and lay down on the ground beneath it to pray. At last I had found a time and place to *be still*. Just as I started to pray, Peanut, our Labrador retriever, landed on my stomach, all fifty pounds of her. I tried rolling away from her but she wouldn't let me; she was determined to lick me on the face. I tried sitting up, holding my knees, and burying my head in my lap, but she got right behind me and breathed down my neck with hot, slobbery, stinking dog breath that brought back memories of a blind date I once had.

"You win, Peanut," I said, and walked back toward the house, remembering an incident from the previous Sunday. We were at church and my brother was trying to lead prayer while holding his squirmy two-year-old in his arms. I was standing next to them when I detected a note of frustration in my brother's voice. I opened one eye to see what was the matter and almost burst out laughing. His head was bowed, his eyes were closed—and his son's pudgy finger was stuck up his father's nose.

I guess with kids and dogs it makes more sense to pray with your eyes wide open.

There are seasons of our life when finding the time for prayer and a place for solitude may seem like the impossible dream, but it isn't. We just may have to work at it a little harder than someone with a more sedentary lifestyle.

For example, we live close to a toll road that connects us with a neighboring community where my husband works and three of my five children attend school. Often I make several trips a day back and forth, chauffeuring kids to school or ball practice. One day as I handed my change to the lady in the booth, she looked at me with concern. "Honey, this is the third time you've gotten on this road in one morning. Don't you know if you're coming or going?"

I just smiled and drove on. My time alone in my

van is well spent. It's one of the few times when I'm still enough to pray.

Think about your schedule and decide when it's easiest for you to be still and reflect. For me it's when I'm walking or driving, the first few minutes of the morning before I get the children up for school, or after I get them to bed at night. I've also learned to keep a Bible or book in the van so when I have unexpected waiting time I can read.

After you decide when the best time is to pray, make it a habit. When I get in the car, I automatically buckle my seat belt and start to pray (and no, I'm *not* praying about my driving skills, although my brother would assure you that I need to).

I have learned *when* I can pray and I know *how* to pray, but it's the last step of prayer that gives me trouble: the letting go of my worries. It took a squirrel to remind me what can happen when we carry our burdens.

My daughter and I were driving through town one day when a squirrel darted in front of our van. I did a double take when I realized the object in this mouth wasn't an oversized nut; it was an apple. The ambitious creature proceeded to run to a tree and climb it, but the weight of the fruit flipped him over backwards and he fell to the ground.

Later, the squirrel came to mind when I realized we had something in common: I handle my problems the same way he does. I carry them around even when they are too big for me to handle on my own.

Jesus said, "Come to me, all you who are weary and burdened, and I will give you rest" (Matthew 11:28, NIV). There is a place where we can lay our burdens down and that place is at our Savior's feet.

An equally important part of prayer is what my sister-in-law refers to as having an "attitude of gratitude." Every morning give thanks for the blessing of another day. Throughout the day take note of the many gifts God has given you: your job; your relationships with family, friends, or colleagues; the spring flowers in your garden; the birds gathering at your feeder.

Don't take your blessings for granted—let God know how much you appreciate all he has done for you.

Be still. Pray. Praise. Spend time with God.

A Prayer for God's Peace

Lord, make me a channel of your peace.

Where there is hatred, let me bring love.

Where there is offense, forgiveness.

Where there is discord, reconciliation.

Where there is doubt, faith.

Where there is despair, hope.

Where there is sadness, joy.

Where there is darkness, your light.

If we give, we are made rich.

If we forget ourselves, we find peace.

If we forgive, we receive forgiveness.

If we die, we receive eternal resurrection.

Give us peace, Lord.

Francis of Assisi

DEstressors

Identifying Your Stress Points and Developing a Plan of Action

1. Are your problems like pizza dough? Do you throw them up in the air, only to catch and release them again and again? List the three problems you are most likely to catch after you release them. Intentionally pray about each problem by name.

2. Think about the moments in your life when you are still. Is there a pattern? Can you create a habit out of those peaceful moments?

3. Do you need to change anything in your routine to enable you to pray daily?

4. At the end of the day, think about what you are most grateful for that day and also the things that have become burdens to you. Gives thanks for the good things. And as you rest at night, remember Jesus' offer to carry your burdens for you.

A Little Effort—A Big Reward

God does not lay a great burden on us—

> *a little thinking of him,*
> *a little adoration,*
> *sometimes to pray for grace,*
> *sometimes to offer him your sorrows,*
> *sometimes to thank him for the good things*
>   *he does.*

Lift up your heart to him even at meals and when you are in company. The least little remembrance will always be acceptable to him. You don't have to be loud. He is nearer to us than you think.

You don't have to be in church all the time in order to be with God. We can make a chapel in our heart where we can withdraw from time to time and converse with him in meekness, humility, and love.

Brother Lawrence

Valerie's Story

My Daily Routine of Prayer and Reflection

O*n waking:* I greet the Lord. Not being
a morning person, I ask him to send his Spirit to
energize and invigorate me to help me make this a
great day. (This really works. It gets me out of bed
in a positive frame of mind, determined to meet
all my challenges with cheer.) Then, at the first
convenient break in our household's morning bus-
tle, I enter into prayer as I also do a stretch routine, eyes closed. (This gentle mind-body regimen
keeps me focused and encourages meditation.) I
always begin with the same prayer: I ask the Lord
to protect our home throughout the day and keep
the five of us from all harm, physical and moral. I
also ask that he reveal his will for us and send his
spirit to help us to do it. Next, I pray for my husband and ask for whatever he might need at the
moment—courage, wisdom, endurance, faith. After that, I pray for family and friends. Then I ask
that my writing that day will be pleasing to the
Lord. As I conclude my stretches, I close my prayer
by giving thanks for our many blessings.

On going to work: When I sit down at the computer, before beginning my writing assignment
for the day, I log onto several Internet sites that
provide me with encouragement and insight into

the Christian life. The first is The Saint of the Day at *www.saints.catholic.org*. I enjoy reading about ordinary people who, afire with an extraordinary love of God, were able to accomplish remarkable things. They remind me that with faith, all things are truly possible. The next site I check out is the Christian Quotation of the Day at *www.gospel com.net/cqod*. Brief, but packed with wisdom and truth, these excerpts of writings by the great Christian thinkers increase my appreciation for my faith heritage and its timelessness. They provide the perfect foundation from which to launch into my day's writing.

Throughout the day: I try to remember to give thanks, especially when an idea appears to help me over a hurdle in my writing. I truly believe those ideas are gifts from God.

When driving: Okay, I'll be honest. Sometimes I wish I had a rocket launcher attached to my front bumper. Since I could easily be a Type A driver, I begin to pray when I sense smoke is about to stream from my ears. Reciting repetitive prayers is tremendously calming.

In the evenings: I treadmill for close to an hour.

Before retiring: Sometimes I do more stretching and meditation before bed, sometimes I read the Bible or another book. One of the saints I read about made a nightly habit of examining his conscience, assessing his faith-walk each day. I like to do the same, so I know what I need to work on and what I need to pray for help with.

Setting aside the personal detail, what remains as important, I think, is the establishment of habits of faith that will see you through those days when everything that can go wrong, does. Our society tends to disdain regimen as destructive of creativity and self-expression. But I've always found the opposite to be true, that adhering to a routine— not for its own sake but in the interest of achieving a greater good—actually facilitates growth. In the arena of faith, it's certainly no exception.

Valerie Kirkwood (novelist)

What Other Women Have to Say

Comments on Breaking the Stress Barrier

The most important way of dealing with stress, for me, is prayer. The hardest part, however, is leaving the burden with God once I have prayed about it. I tend to keep wanting to carry it around. I try to find the good in everything and concentrate on that as opposed to the bad, to seize each moment and make the most of it. Keeping busy with all the normal, mundane chores even helps at times.

—*Connie (mother and teacher)*

I can talk to everyone and anyone here on earth when I'm faced with stress in my life, but no one— and I mean no one—can help me like God when I talk to him in prayer. When I give my problems to him, a sense of peace comes over me. My advice is to pray, pray some more, and keep praying.

—*Laura (age 30)*

Last year my daughter was involved in a terrible accident. A car hit her as she was walking on a crosswalk on her college campus. I prayed on the way to the hospital. At that time I didn't think she was seriously hurt. But upon my arrival, I learned that she had been thrown backward on her head by the truck. She was on a respirator in an induced coma. It was very disconcerting to see her with her eyes open but completely still and giving no reaction to any stimulation.

I called a friend to ask for prayer and she came right over to be with me for a while. And at the same time, I had the feeling that God knew all about the situation, and I didn't have to consciously pray because he was there and realized everything without my saying anything. I felt that I was "blanketed" by his care and concern and by the prayers and concern of others. I felt that since I feel his presence in my life every day, there was an unseen calming presence all around me. I cannot even imagine what it would be like to feel that I was alone, without God.

—*Laura Kay (teacher , mother, and grandmother)*

When I am stressed I pray to God to help me. If it is possible, I close my eyes and imagine I am in a forest, next to a small waterfall. I listen to the water running over the rocks and picture a small clear stream with a cool breeze blowing.

—*Margaret (wife, mother, and grandmother)*

I arise for "quiet" time. I read Scripture and pray, go outside and reflect. The early morning is the most beautiful time of the day. My head is clear, the phone hasn't started ringing, and I feel as though I have the whole world to myself.

—*Cora (age 57, retired postal worker)*

Maximize the Positive, Minimize the Negative

A strong positive mental attitude will create more miracles than any wonder drug.

Patricia Neal

Happiness is largely under our control. It is a battle to be waged and not a feeling to be awaited.

Dennis Prager

For we can hold on to [God's] promise with confidence. This confidence is like a strong and trustworthy anchor for our souls.

Hebrews 6:18-19, NLT

Sooner or later all of us are bound to hit a pothole while motoring down the highway of life. Over the years I've tried to look at things objectively and ask myself, "Now is this really a problem or just an inconvenience?" Most of the time it's an inconvenience. I have learned that

I have to make a conscious effort to maximize the positive and minimize the negative.

When our oldest child was born, my pediatrician gave me some wonderful advice. She said, "Catch him being good and praise him. The more you reward good behavior, the less he will behave inappropriately." During the seven years I taught at the local high school, I thought about her advice frequently, especially when I had troubled children in my classroom. *Why,* I wondered, *is it so easy to notice their bad behavior and so hard to recognize and reward their good behavior?*

The same advice my pediatrician gave me applies to spouses as well. This is what Mattie, a friend of mine, told me about her husband:

Dave and I have been married for thirty years, and in all those years he has never once taken notice of any redecorating I do around the house. Sometimes I think I could take every stick of furniture out, change the carpet, and replace it with all new furniture, and he'd never notice. I wish he'd compliment me on how hard I work to make our home look nice. It really bugs me that he cares so little about his surroundings. But on the other hand, he never complains about how much I spend. I know women whose husbands would have a fit if they came home and there were new curtains in the den. Not Dave. He says money isn't as important to him as I am and if it makes me happy, he's happy.

When it comes to her marriage, Mattie's learned how to overlook the negative and focus on the positive.

The week I signed the contract to write this book my husband became ill, my son broke his foot, the dishwasher flooded the kitchen, the washer stained my clothes brown, the dryer started making weird noises and eating socks, and the pipes beneath the kitchen sink developed a leak, spewing water out onto the hardwood floor. For months I had asked God to bless my writing endeavors. But now that I finally had the contract in my hand, I found it hard to do a victory dance while standing knee deep in dirty laundry in a kitchen full of unwashed dishes.

Life is full of complications and some are more complex than others. You can't change the circumstances, but you *can* change you attitude. How? Well, for starters, you can assess your friendships. Look at the people you choose to be your friends. Do they constantly focus on the negative? Are they pessimists? If the answer to that question is yes, then chances are good that you will be, too.

Do you consistently read books or watch movies that depress or upset you? Then it is likely you will reflect the attitudes you see in those materials, because "'bad company corrupts good character'" (1 Corinthians 15:33, NLT). However, if you "fix your thoughts on what is true and honorable and right" and "think about things that are pure and lovely and admirable," things that are "excellent and worthy of praise" (Philippians 4:8, NLT), then your attitude will change. You will be lifted up.

How do you *lift* yourself up?

I asked this question once at a women's retreat and smiled when someone on the front row whispered, "I bought a Wonder bra."

I bought one too, but it didn't work. I had to take it back when I started hyperventilating. The thing was so tight it made my eyeballs pop out. I returned it, but I had misplaced the receipt, so I asked the sales lady if she would still refund my money or if I needed to try a different size. She looked me up and down, batted her eyes, leaned over the counter, and whispered, "Honey, these are Wonder bras, not Miracle bras. Have you ever thought about implants?"

That's a silly example, but it holds some truth. There are books and movies and friends (and even fun little "luxuries" we can give ourselves along the way) that make us feel good about ourselves and the world God created. Those are the things we should use to lift ourselves up.

On the light side, some of my personal favorite "lifts" are the books by Erma Bombeck. I also like to read about Mother Teresa and Helen Keller, and I adore all the Chicken Soup books.

Then there's the best inspirational book of all time: the Bible. Study the lives of Jesus, Abraham, Ruth and Naomi, Moses, Paul, Stephen, Peter, and John to inspire you when you are down. Look at your problems and compare them to their problems. Then look at the way they handled stress. What you learn may change more than your attitude—it might just change your life.

As we look at life's stress factors and consider our attitudes, we should also keep in mind that hormonal changes can mysteriously affect our mood and mindset. That doesn't mean we should use PMS or menopause as an excuse when we're in a bad mood (the *P* in PMS doesn't stand for permanent—even though I've known some women who thought it did), but it does mean that we should factor in those changes. When the attitude you want is *not* the attitude that's coming out, give yourself some slack. Relax.

Not long ago I decided to try and explain these hormonal changes to my husband, Bill. He was sitting in his usual spot in the den going through his nighttime ritual: channel surfing with the remote. I launched into a detailed explanation of mood swings and bloating. I suspected he wasn't listening by the glazed television stare on his face, so I put my hands on my hips, glared down at him and asked him if he'd heard any of what I had just said.

"Yes, dear, I heard you," he answered automatically without bothering to look up, "but Primestar doesn't carry PMS."

Forget Mars. Sometimes my husband is from Pluto.

It's not only hormones that affect our attitudes. Our ability to be content affects us. And we can't just be content on demand, either. Being content is especially difficult these days, because we're led to believe that having more is always better, and we often feel we have a right to demand more.

An issue of *Gospel Minutes* describes this problem:

> The days of single car garages, black and white
> television, small closets and no air conditioning
> in homes or cars have been replaced with televi-
> sions in two or more rooms, walk-in closets, va-
> cation homes, and the desire to have more.
> Meanwhile we are pressured to provide . . .
> money for our medical needs and retirement in-
> vestments so that we are not a burden . . . when
> we get older. With all these demands it is no
> wonder that many people consider a successful
> life making a good living. But is that real suc-
> cess?
> Sadly what we think will make us successful
> can poison [us]. . . . While we spend our time
> making money, we may be ruining what is more
> important. What woman wants written on [her]
> tombstone, "I wish I could spend one more
> hour at the office?"

We need to rework our attitudes and our goals, so
that like the apostle Paul we can say, "I have
learned how to get along happily whether I have
much or little" (Philippians 4:11, NLT).

My grandmother is eighty-five years old, and I
love the way she describes discontentment. "Our
wants are many, but our needs are few," she says.

There is clearly nothing wrong with wanting to
better ourselves—it's what a life of faith in God is
all about. But when always wanting more nega-

tively affects our attitude, we need to consider a change.

Even when we are happy, many of us are afraid to show it. We treat happiness as if it were a big diamond ring in a bad neighborhood: we don't dare flash it around because someone might see it and snatch it out of our grasp.

Many of life's lessons I learned the hard way during my mother's illness and subsequent death from colon cancer. One lesson I learned was about fear of joy. When Mama became too ill to teach school, she longed for her classroom and her students. By the time she finally admitted that she wouldn't be going back to work, she was too weak and too sick to clean out her classroom, so I did it for her. It was one of the hardest things I've ever done in my life, especially when I realized all the wadded up pieces of paper in her desk drawers were appreciation notes from former sixth grade students.

"Mrs. Bell, You r a gud teecher and I lub you," one note read. "Mrs. Bell, I am mad at you. Your friend, Donna P.S. Can I borrow a nickle at recess?" And on and on. Mama loved teaching almost as much as she loved her students, and I know her career brought her great joy. But that wasn't the part of her work she shared with me most often. Usually I heard about early morning bus duty, lunch room food, the ancient heating and cooling system in her building—whatever it was that wasn't going right.

One afternoon near the end of her life, I found

Mama outside sitting in the swing beneath the large crimson maple tree. She was staring off into space, and when I asked her what she was thinking about she replied in a whisper, "I was just thinking how beautiful everything is and how very much I don't want to leave it."

Mama was right (as she was about most things). The world is beautiful and it can vanish in the blink of an eye. None of us knows how many tomorrows we have, and if we wait for everything in our life to be perfect in order to be happy, we may never be happy.

For less stress, learn to maximize the positive and minimize the negative.

DEstressors

Identifying Your Stress Points and Developing a Plan of Action

1. *Attitude check:* What three daily life situations can cause your attitude to become negative? List five things you can do to maximize the positive aspects of your life. (Here are some you might consider: read a psalm of hope before meeting with that impatient work colleague; give yourself a little treat after running stressful errands; read a book that promises to give you an attitude boost.)

2. What would you answer if someone asked you, "Are you happy?" If not yes, what stands between you and happiness? Name those things and then ask a friend to help you come up with creative ways to develop contentment and hope in specific areas.

3. Make a list of all the positives in your life. Keep it posted where you can see it and give God a big thank you every time you look at it.

4. Pray for patience and joy. During stressful times, it's hard to remember the wonderful possibilities the future (and the present) holds, but prayer can help keep things in perspective.

Jenny's Story

What My Daughter Taught Me about Joy

In my life I have had a few big blows. But I can't think of any situation, no matter how terrible it seemed at the time, that I wish never happened. This is why: In those hard times, God always carried me through. I figure that God knows what is best for me in the terrible times, and he has a plan. He's always brought me through the bad times and he always takes care of me.

After I married Shane, we had a beautiful little girl, Shelby. Then I became pregnant again. Near the end of this second pregnancy, the doctors detected something wrong on the ultrasound. Within the space of just a few days, my world was completely turned upside down. The doctors told me there were going to be major problems with this baby, so Shane and I did our best to prepare ourselves.

Our second daughter, Sydney, was born on Easter Sunday. Her condition was so rare and unique that it was several weeks before the diagnosis was official, and even since then it's been changed to a different form of the original diagnosis. She has an extremely rare genetic condition called x-linked chondrodysplasia, which is a form of dwarfism with multiple complications.

Here I was, in the hospital, surrounded by mothers with newborns. People were coming to congratulate the other mothers and bringing gifts, but when people came to my room, no one knew what to say. The chaplain came and asked me if I wanted last rites. Sydney's prognosis at that point was so bad they thought she might not make it.

I hate to admit this, but for the first three weeks of her life, I resented my baby. I wish now I could change the way I felt, but at the time I couldn't. Then something happened that totally changed my perspective.

A pregnant friend of mine was at her doctor's office, and while she was there the doctor lost the baby's heart beat. One minute it was there, and the next, nothing. She was almost ready to deliver, and for some unknown reason the baby suddenly died.

A few days later the baby was buried. I went to the funeral. She was a beautiful little girl, tiny and pink, and she was lying in the smallest casket I'd ever seen. Right then and there I knew it was time to quit feeling sorry for myself. God had given me the opportunity to hold my daughter, to nurse her, and to love her. My friend would never get that opportunity.

Sydney is almost two years old now and we've both come so far. She's doing so much more than the doctors ever said she would that she amazes them.

And my husband and I have come to love and cherish her as a special gift from God.

People look at Sydney and see her handicaps and they ask me how I do it, as if I have some secret to share with them, which I don't. I'm just like everyone else. I'm just Shelby and Sydney's mom, and I take one problem at a time, one day at a time.

It helps me to deal with Sydney's problems when I remember a story I read about a father who had a handicapped son. When the son was grown, his father said to him, "Son, everyone is handicapped, yours are just a little more visible than most people's." That's what I'm going to tell Sydney when she's grown.

If Sydney had to be born the way she is, I'm so very thankful that God chose me to be her mother. The world is full of people who would have listened to the doctors and immediately institutionalized her and given up without even trying. I appreciate the medical advice the doctors gave me initially, but they only told us the terrible things that could happen with Sydney. They didn't tell us about all the joy she would bring into our lives.

I've come a long way. I still have my moments, but I really don't get too stressed over things anymore, because I found a way to deal with it and it's the most simple thing in the world: I just give it up to God and eat chocolate!

Jenny (property appraiser, wife,
and mother of two daughters)

Sandra's Story

A Change of Heart

Ever since my husband and I got married, we had dreamed of living in Colorado. But when an arson fire burned our religious publishing business to the ground (depriving us of an income and forcing us to leave our much loved home in Denver and move to Oklahoma), having an optimistic attitude became a challenge for me.

The day we moved into our Tulsa house, the heat soared to 105 degrees, and the air conditioner was broken. About the same time, I turned forty, and found out I was pregnant with our sixth child.

For the first time in my life, I wrestled with depression. While we ran a little Christian bookstore and struggled to put our publishing business back together, we attended a congregation that had a membership of several thousand members. It was a church in which it was easy to float on the surface and not get involved, if that's what you chose. And at that low point in my life, that was my choice. We faithfully attended but didn't have a friend in the entire congregation.

Then, to our shock, the Internal Revenue Service arrived with a surprise: The religious bookstore we had been allowed to take over for almost nothing to help us get back on our feet owed many thousands of dollars in back taxes. As the new owners, we were responsible. A lien was slapped on every remaining thing we owned.

About this time, my attitude bottomed out. I even went to the library and checked out books on depression to try to fix my dismal mood, but nothing seemed to work.

Then one day, a lady I barely knew approached me at church about helping her with a baby shower. I politely refused, making up some spur-of-the-moment excuse. Not to be deterred, she next began to urge me to help her teach one of the congregation's Bible studies. Although I resisted, she finally got me to agree to at least sit in and "help" her with it.

As we studied together in preparation for the weekly class, I confessed to my new friend that I still felt totally alone in the congregation and knew almost no one.

"That's easy to fix," she said. "We will have a coffee! Just start down the church directory and call names until you find ten women who don't have outside jobs and will agree to come," she continued. "We'll have it at your house, since it's bigger; but I'll bring the coffee and doughnuts."

Somewhat aghast at what I had committed to, I gave her plan a half-hearted try. To my surprise, I easily found ten women who were eager to get acquainted. In fact, we had such a good time that we planned another coffee with ten more women for the next week. Soon I knew many women in the congregation, and I became very busy and happy—again.

In our very next Bible study, this verse from Proverbs 27 came up: "As iron sharpens iron, a friend sharpens a friend" (v. 17, NLT). Had it not been for my persistent friend, I might still be moping about in my grumpy attitude. Never again have I taken the need for friends lightly.

Sandra (wife, mother, grandmother, magazine editor)

What Other Women Have to Say

Comments on Breaking the Stress Barrier

I like to read biographies about people who were very successful. I learn their methods of dealing with stress and it helps me realize that my problems are very small compared to everyone else's. I also feel less stress if my home and office are neat and tidy. Heaped up papers and dishes feel like they are on my head.

Heather (pension plan director, single)

I keep inspirational tapes in my car. So when I commute to work or wherever, I listen to songs of praise to the One who has blessed me in so many ways.

Vickie (bank teller, wife, and mother)

My husband works with the young people in our church, and I help him as much as possible: we're a team. There are so many issues facing teenagers today. Since I do not have children, I don't know *all* of the problems parents face, but I do know that parents play a huge part in how their children turn out. So many families are so busy with sports and activities that they don't place emphasis on *spiritual* training.

Parents are working to provide more "things" for their children, but they aren't seeking the kingdom of God. This disturbs me because if they would put God first, they wouldn't have to work so hard at seeking fulfillment elsewhere: God provides.

Rachel (wife and counselor)

Avoid the Problems You Can

Learn to see in another's calamity the ills which you should *avoid*.

Publius Syrus

My dear brothers and sisters[,] watch out for people who cause divisions and upset people's faith by teaching things that are contrary to what you have been taught. Stay away from them.

Romans 16:17, NLT

Run away from infantile indulgence. Run after mature righteousness—faith, love, peace—joining those who are in honest and serious prayer before God. Refuse to get involved in inane discussions; they always end up in fights. God's servant must not be argumentative, but a gentle listener and a teacher who keeps cool.

2 Timothy 2:23-25, THE MESSAGE

Some things are unavoidable at this point in my life: mountains of laundry, endless trips to the grocery store, and my kids' fearless determination to test the outer limits of my patience. Not long ago, they did just that. We were on our way to my aunt's house for a barbecue, when I noticed a strange smell in the van.

"Have you guys been stuffing your dirty socks under the seats again?" I asked.

"Mom, even their socks don't smell this bad," my daughter said as she pinched the end of her nose in disgust and rolled her window down.

"You're right. OK, I'll give you a dollar if you'll get down on your hands and knees and find the source of the smell." (Normally, I insist everyone wear seat belts at all times, but this was an emergency.)

"You're on," my daughter said, and she began crawling through the van.

It wasn't long before her bloodcurdling scream told me she'd found what she was looking for.

"Pull over," she ordered.

"What is it?"

"Just pull over!" she yelled.

When I saw what she had found, I knew why she wanted me to stop the van. The boys had left their fishing bait (chicken livers) under the seat, and during the course of the 100-degree day, the mix had simmered until it was cooked somewhere between medium-well and well-done.

After we had disposed of the putrid smelling box and Rachel had composed herself once more, I pulled back onto the highway. I pulled a dollar bill from my purse and handed it to Rachel.

"Next time I'll take no less than a five," she muttered.

I can't say as I blame her.

Life is full of surprises, some are welcome and some aren't (cooked liver belongs in the *aren't* category). Some problems we can foresee and some we can't. Why not make your life a little easier by staying away from the stressors you can avoid?

There are some danger spots to watch out for such as, *strife*. *Strife* and *stress* go together to clutter and confuse our lives. What is it that causes you strife? Is it giving in to a weakness you know can lead to frustration and hurt?

Take this test (I know this will sound like those word problems you used to get in math class, but bear with me): If you have ten dollars in your checking account and a friend calls and invites you to go shopping with her, do you go? (Strife potential is high here because if she spends money, you will probably want to do the same. But being broke is a bigger stressor.)

Or this test: You are on a diet and are trying to exercise every day by walking to work. Which route would you take, the one that goes directly in front of the bakery or the longer one that doesn't? (I know which is the most tempting—but won't you be glad when you get home calorie free?)

Proverbs 4:25-27 says, "Look straight ahead, and fix your eyes on what lies before you. Mark out a straight path for your feet; then stick to the path and stay safe. Don't get side-tracked" (NLT). Use this verse to help you mark your path in order to steer clear of temptations. Ask yourself if any of the following are obstacles that might slow you down. If so, then *avoiding* them might be the answer.

- *Procrastination.* Putting things off to the last minute is something we all do from time to time, but if you find that you're a habitual procrastinator, don't put it off any longer, tackle those projects! It's time to make some changes. Here are a few steps that can make the difference.

- *Excuses.* If you find that you are prone to making excuses, learn to replace those excuses with motivational thoughts like, *There's no time like the present,* or *the sooner I get this done, the sooner I can do something else* or *I will feel great when this task is accomplished.*

- *Discouragement.* Try to tackle the task at hand by dividing it into smaller parts. If it's a big job, this will really help you feel like it's not so overwhelming and it's easy to manage.

- *Low morale.* When you have finished a task, give yourself a pat on the back or give yourself a special treat.

- *Forgetfulness.* Remember that feeling of self-satisfaction and go for it the next time there is something on your agenda that needs to be done without delay.

- *Stimulants.* I know those of you who are big coffee klatchers aren't going to like this one bit, but caffeine (especially during menstruation)—as well as high doses of sugar—can create stress and strife in your body without your even realizing it. These substances create highs and lows in your body that tie directly into mood-swings, creating an unstable environment for your emotions. Cutting those down—or even out—can make a big difference in your physical health as well as your moods.

When you avoid the big stressors in your life—the ones that you *can* avoid—you gain control and a sense of balance, which, in turn, can help you with those stressors you *can't* control . . . like the chicken livers in the van!

DEstressors

Identifying Your Stress Points and Developing a Plan of Action

1. List three things that continually cause you strife that you have a sneaking suspicion could be avoided. Now read Proverbs 4:25-27 again: "Look straight ahead, and fix your eyes on what lies before you. Mark out a straight path for your feet; then stick to the path and stay safe. Don't get sidetracked" (NLT).

   For each of the three things you listed, brainstorm for positive and creative ways to mark out—and stick to— a straight path.

2. If you feel overwhelmed by problems that seem avoidable, but you don't know *how* to begin avoiding them, remember that God wants to help you find your way through this dark night. Bring yourself to him. Ask for help with these issues. In the book of James it says, "If you need wisdom—if you want to know what God wants you to do—ask him, and he will gladly tell

you. He will not resent your asking"
(1:5, NLT).

Lisa's Story

Avoid Overcommitting Yourself

If possible, remove as many things as you can from your life that cause stress. Some, of course, are immovable. But if you can remove the others, you can deal with the "permanent" ones better.

We all have stressors in our lives that we are unable to eliminate: work, children to take care of, a house to clean, etc. There are usually many other stressors, though, that we *can* eliminate if we choose to do so.

I am a very active member of our church, as well as active in several civic organizations and the school PTA. There are some times when I have had to learn to say no to potential obligations associated with church, school, and community. For example, in a year in which I was committee chairman for a PTA function and also in charge of a large Bible study at our church, I had to say no to other committees or special events. I can only stretch myself so far. It has proven to be in my and my family's best interest for me to limit my obligations and to try to do those well.

The way I am trying to decrease stress from my Immovable Stressors list is to put the things I have to do in perspective. Our family lives a basically organized life, but sometimes chaos can occur. When items get broken, like a vase or a dish, I remind myself of my husband's saying, "They make them every day." If a child needs help with homework but I need to clean the house, I remind myself that the dust will still be there when we are through studying.

I've also learned that sometimes relationships can cause stress on our lives. Obviously, you can't remove your children, spouse, coworkers or neighbors, but you can change your attitude toward these people. Sometimes relationships can actually be improved by giving space to other people in your life. Because I am not a perfect person, I must not expect others to be perfect but instead love them for who they are and control my negative reactions to them.

The best way for me to try to reduce stress is to learn to say no when necessary, to keep things in perspective, and to love and accept people in my life as they are. In every area of life, prayer helps me. God can and will effectively help us to deal with stress when we turn our lives over to him.

Lisa (35, wife, mother, engineer)

Kim's Story

Avoiding Things That Trigger Negative Physical Reactions

I have hypoglycemia—low blood sugar. Most people's blood sugar is between 80 and 120. When I have mine tested after fasting, it can get into the low range: 35–45. The biggest concern for people with this condition is that it can lead to diabetes.

Whenever I am late in eating, or I eat too much sugar, I get the shakes. Then it is much easier for me to lose my temper. My husband often notices a change in my personality before I realize that my sugar level is getting off and affecting my mood. I remember one time we went with friends to a restaurant for dinner and I did not realize how far away the place was. By the time I got there, I was extremely upset. It really bothers me to lose control of my emotions but sometimes *when* I eat is not within my control. I try to anticipate potential problems and take along a snack (peanut butter works well) if I am not sure when I will be able to eat.

I am also allergic to perfume and almost every scent people use today. Besides making me feel bad physically, this can also cause a lot of stress. I have arrived at baby or bridal showers in friends' homes only to be forced to leave because their houses smelled too good.

But I try to adjust. For example, in church, I sit in an aisle seat because there's room to move if someone wearing too much perfume sits close to me. At ladies' retreats, I try to plan carefully who I stay with, because even if my friend doesn't wear perfume, her scented body lotion can have the same effect on me. So, I have to be constantly aware of what I smell. A small amount of perfume or scented lotion can make my eyes water, nose run and head hurt for a long time. I will have to deal with this the rest of my life. I can take medicine (when I am not pregnant) to help control my allergies, but it does not make the problem go away.

Another problem I had was sleep apnea. When my medical doctor kept asking me how I was sleeping at night and recommending I go see a sleep doctor, I kept telling him that the only reason I was tired was because I was the mother of a two-year-old—eventually, I told him, I would get enough sleep.

I almost canceled my appointment with the sleep doctor because I thought it was a waste of time and money. Fortunately, I went. I spent two nights in a sleep lab and learned that I stopped breathing so often that I was waking up thirty times an hour. No wonder I was always sleepy! At the age of twenty-eight, I had major surgery on my nose and throat to remove excessive tissue. The surgery worked for me and a lot of my stress went away.

I would advise every woman who feels she isn't handling stress well to get a thorough physical examination. The problem very well could be something you're totally unaware of.

Kim (wife and mother)

What Other Women Have to Say

Comments on Breaking the Stress Barrier

I find that when I eat a lot of sweets, I don't cope as well. There seems to be a connection to mood swings.

Carol (college professor)

When I drink too much coffee, my nerves get jangled and I become tense. When that happens I am much more likely to lose my temper—and that causes even more stress!

Tabitha (wife and mother)

If I eat too much during the holidays not only do I gain weight, but I also feel depressed over my lack of self-control.

Pat (social worker)

Share Your Troubles

Share each other's troubles and problems, and in this way obey the law of Christ.

Galatians 6:2, NLT

It seems to me that trying to live without friends is like milking a bear to get cream for your morning coffee. It is a whole lot of trouble, and then not worth much after you get it.

Zora Neale Hurston

While such friends are near us we feel that all is well. The influence of their calm, mellow natures is a libation poured upon our discontent, and we feel its healing touch as the ocean feels the mountain stream freshening its brine.

Helen Keller, adapted

The ornament of a house are the friends who frequent it.

Ralph Waldo Emerson

Think of ways to encourage one another to outbursts of love and good deeds.

Hebrews 10:24, NLT

During the busiest seasons of our lives, it is often difficult to spend time with our friends. Just finding the time to talk on the phone is next to impossible.

When my children were very young, there was always one of them in need of my attention, especially when I received a telephone call. I could always count on a squabble or a minor crisis to interrupt my conversation. Since then things have improved somewhat, but now finding a time when the phone line is available—and I am awake enough to make a call—is next to impossible.

One night this week my friend Annette called. I was on my way out the door to my son's basketball game, so I told her I would return her call later. When we arrived back home, it was too late to call, so I waited until the next morning. The moment I heard her groggy voice I knew I'd woken her up. I tried again that night, but by the time my two teenagers finished conducting their marathon phone sessions, she was asleep again. The next day she called me from her car phone as I was walking out the door to go pick up the boys at school. We made a tentative luncheon date for the next week, but on that day one of my children was ill, and I had to cancel. If Annette and I both weren't determined to keep our friendship alive, it would never survive, but because we love each other and enjoy each other's company, we keep working at it. We've been friends since high school, so we share the past, but we also value the times we presently share, and we look forward to a time when we can get together more often.

Sadly, some of my other friendships haven't done as well. I placed them on the back burner to simmer, only to come back to them and find the pot was empty. I didn't attend to them, and they disappeared.

Friendships are a blessing—and are not to be taken for granted. Here, my pal Beth describes the importance of friendship:

Just gossiping with a friend over something that is making me crazy helps me vent and put it in perspective. My girlfriends always affirm me by saying things like, "I know just what you mean. That's happened to me too. I often feel that way." They don't offer solutions—most of the time I know what needs to be done—they just let me know that I am not alone, and I'm not crazy. And that takes my stress levels down considerably.

They also physically jump in to help when necessary. I remember one incident clearly: My entire family was scheduled to go away on vacation, but then my father became ill. We couldn't get our money back so we decided that we would go anyway, without my mother and father. I didn't know how seriously ill Dad was yet, but I knew it was bad. I felt horrible about leaving Mom with this mess for two weeks and couldn't make up my mind whether I should go or not. Mostly I was concerned that Mom wouldn't take care of herself and wouldn't eat.

My neighborhood friends told me to go and they would watch over her. I went, feeling a little bit better about it. I found out later that when my friends cooked their own dinners, they made up extra and brought it to my mother. By doing this, they allowed me to get a much needed break and get through a really rotten time. I will always be grateful for this. They not only helped me in a stressful situation but also made me realize how important being connected is to reducing stress. When you are part of a community, when you are part of something that is much larger than just you, there comes a comfort and sense of well-being that is instrumental in reducing stress. When I can do the same sort of helping things for my friends, I feel the same calm and joy that I did in receiving such help.

It's this kind of support—given and received—that I've experienced with my sister-in-law Kelly. We have found that leaning on each other makes us stronger. Over the years I've come to believe that God sent Kelly as the answer to my prayers.

About a year ago we decided that it would help us relieve stress if once a month we had a girls' night out. At first it was just a few of us going out to dinner, but word began to spread. Last month we had a van load of women, all anxious for a few hours of conversation about something other than football or homework. Who knows? By next month we may even have to charter a bus.

A girls' night out not only relieves stress but also gives us something to look forward to when life gets a little crazy. When I have a problem, Kelly is one of the first people to know about it. When she has a problem she calls me, or if she can't call, she has one of her children call for her.

Last month her seven-year-old son, Thomas, called and said, "Aunt Teresa, Mama needs your help."

"What's wrong?" I asked, picturing all sorts of catastrophes.

"The washing machine blowed up and rained in the basement until the ceiling fell in," he said calmly.

I slammed the phone down, grabbed Russell and Grant, the twins, and hurried to her house. On the way there, Russell said, "Oh shoot, Grant. We forgot our tool box."

"That's okay," Grant replied. "Thomas has got a chain saw."

I tried to visualize what they planned to do with a chain saw, but decided not to stress about it—after all, I hadn't yet seen exactly what we were dealing with. Maybe Thomas was exaggerating when he called.

He wasn't. I rang the doorbell and he and his little brother, Price, appeared wearing orange life vests.

Solemn-faced Thomas opened the door and said, "Mama's in the basement. She says, 'Hurry.'"

There is a John Denver song that says "some days are diamonds, some days are stones. Some days the hard times won't leave us alone." When you are given a diamond, share it with a friend and it will shine brighter. And when it rains in your basement, let a friend help keep you afloat.

DEstressors

Identifying Your Stress Points and Developing a Plan of Action

1. List three friends you see fairly often. Are you and your friends satisfied with the amount of time you see each other? If not, call up each friend and brainstorm for ways you could spend more time together. Perhaps plan a mini-vacation at someone's house—a day spa full of little relaxing treats. Or maybe you have no time to plan a mini-vacation—does your friend need to get a little work done in her garden? Can you help your friend weed her garden in exchange for help painting your garage? That way you can get projects done and still have quality time together. Or, perhaps you can run errands together.

2. Now list three friends that you'd like to reconnect with after not seeing them for a while. I know you're stressed, so you don't have a lot of time to make a get-together work, but how about considering the following simple options?

- If your work is close to a friend's workplace or home, take a lunch break together.

- If you both have kids who play well together, take your families to a park. Bring a thermos of tea to share with your friend and take some time to chit-chat while the kids play.

- If you have a friend at church you'd like to see more often, plan a little time together at the next church banquet, retreat, or community service project.

Diana's Story

The Hand of a Best Friend

> There is a friend who sticks closer than a brother.—*Proverbs 18:24, NKJV*

During the past twenty-one years of my friendship with Connie, our lives have paralleled in ways only God could have ordained.

We met in high school at our first job in a donut shop, and our friendship has been on a roll ever since. Long-distance moves, personality and priority differences, and marriages and careers that took our lives in different directions have challenged our friendship, yet made it even stronger over the years. We became stepparents in the same year—an amazing parallel—and spent countless hours discussing the challenges of our ready-made families.

While I struggled with the emotional pain of stepparenting—my stepson Pierre acted out toward me because of abandonment and abuse issues he had suffered at the hand of his mother—Connie's challenge was the escalating emotional and physical abuse that surfaced a month into her marriage.

In 1997 Connie courageously fled to a women's shelter. She has struggled to divorce herself from domestic violence and regain her sense of self and her personal possessions ever since.

A year later, on my stepson's sixteenth birthday, my husband and I were looking forward to calling him at his mother's place and wishing him a Sweet Sixteen. Before we had a chance to dial, our phone rang with the news that Pierre had gone camping with some friends and spent the night celebrating his birthday with a bottle of vodka an adult had provided. Sometime during the night, a few hours into his sixteenth birthday, Pierre died of alcohol poisoning.

Once again Connie's life and mine had paralleled. Here I was with my world crashing around me. The death I was dealing with and the divorce Connie had dealt with each interrupted our lives and yielded emotional scars and broken dreams.

Through the numbing days that followed, God gave me strength and peace to endure the endless phone calls and funeral preparations. Riding on this emotional calm, I almost protested when Connie called and said God had put it on her heart to fly down for the memorial and funeral service. Although I didn't think her trip necessary and knew it would be a huge financial burden for her, I quietly acquiesced.

God showed me, through Connie, how much I needed her close by. For four days she became an emotional pillar. We hugged, prayed, cried, and took walks. When my emotional and spiritual strength was drained, Connie intuitively knew when to renew my energy with an open ear or a fierce hug. And even through the pain of the funeral and the finality of closing the casket, a God-given calm began to settle over me as Connie reached over and took my hand in hers and I grasped my husband's with the other hand.

"Be strong and of good courage; do not be afraid, nor be dismayed; for the LORD your God is with you wherever you go" (Joshua 1:9, NKJV). God's Word, Jesus' promises, and the hand of my one true friend have carried me through life's unexpected cataclysms. On bended knees we have cried together, and once again, we hold each other's hands with God as our strength.

Diana Kathrein
(38, publisher of Parenting Today's Teen*)*

Leah's Story

Friends Who Don't Forsake You

When my husband, Scott, unexpectedly announced that he wanted a divorce after eight months of marriage, I was shocked—to say the least. I was even more shocked when I discovered that he was having an affair. For weeks, I was hurt, embarrassed, and stunned. I could not eat or sleep and, for some reason, I shook with the chills for a good two weeks.

During all this time, my friends were there for me in many ways—from spending the night with me to forcing me to go out in public with them. They showed me that there was nothing to be embarrassed about, and they reminded me that *not* everything in the world was false and deceptive.

Dad kept telling me that I had great friends, but he also warned me that I should expect some of them to take Scott's side because some of them had been his friends long before they were mine. I braced myself for it, but it never happened. They spent all night trying to explain to him how wrong he was and they defended me. Today I am grateful that we didn't get back together, but at the time it meant the world to me that they would go to so much effort to make things right.

There was not one event that I can say made all the difference, but I can say I am lucky to have a group of friends—male and female—that surrounded me with love and support and gave me the confidence to go back out and face the world with my head up and my eyes open.

Leah (attorney)

Carol's Story

My Best Friend

I consider the Lord to be my very best friend, "a present help in trouble," as it says in the Psalms. After our son was born in 1979, I was told I had fibroid tumors. These tumors continued to grow. That next summer I scheduled a doctor's appointment for an ultrasound. Exploratory surgery was scheduled early the next week. Since my husband had to take care of our five-year-old daughter and our nine-month-old son, I was wheeled into the operating room alone—with no one there to give me encouragement. So, I said to the Lord, "It's just you and me." A very comforting feeling engulfed me. That comfort lingered even while I awaited lab results and while I had a honeydew melon-sized tumor removed.

There's another instance of God's friendship to me. During Christmas of 1972, I contracted the London flu from my fourth-grade students (who had suffered severely from it right before Christmas). During the course of the illness, I became so weak I needed assistance from my husband to walk. My pulse was weak and racing, and I lay supine all day long.

One Friday night, I felt close to death. I was in bed. Everyone else had retired. I desperately wanted to contact my parents but decided they couldn't help.

While lying there, I heard an audible voice that said, "Carol, your heart is going to speed up three times." Suddenly my heart stopped its pounding and became really slow and regular. Then it started beating louder and faster. It then slowed again and repeated this same process two more times. Afterwards, I relished being in a comforting embrace by the Lord, and I fell asleep.

Full recovery of strength took several weeks, but that experience was a definite turning point. Since that experience, I have understood and appreciated God's friendship and care: He is there for us when we rely on Him.

Carol (college professor, wife, and mother)

What Other Women Have to Say

Comments on Breaking the Stress Barrier

My stressless moments are when I'm playing Mexican dominoes with my friends. For several hours, we laugh, eat, and share good conversation. I look forward to that night like a trip to the beach.

Carol (retired teacher)

If I can just "vent" my feelings and problems to someone who will sympathize and listen—without giving advice or opinions—it helps me tremendously!

Barbara (age 52)

I enjoy dropping everything and going to the mall and window shopping, or going out to dinner and a movie with girl friends. We are all usually ready for adult conversations and laugh at the silly "mommy things" we do to entertain our families.

Melanie (wife and stay-at-home mom, age 39)

My friends help me through stressful times by listening patiently as I talk the situation out. They care enough to listen as I vent, analyze the situation, repeat myself, blame others, blame myself, express confusion, and cry. Their willingness to listen and care is the most important gift they ever give me.

What doesn't work is when they try to "fix my problem" for me. Another thing that doesn't work is that I sometimes expect them to offer support in a specific way, and am angry at them when they don't magically know what I need. With my closest friends I am finally learning (sometimes) to ask for what I need: "I need a hug." "I want to talk about my mother's death. Will you listen?" When I am able to ask, they always come through for me.

Sandy (computer programmer, age 39)

Find Strength for the Journey

If we had no winter, the spring would not be so pleasant: if we did not sometimes taste of adversity, prosperity would not be so welcome.

Anne Bradstreet

Give your burdens to the Lord, and he will take care of you. He will not permit the godly to slip and fall.

Psalm 55:22, NLT

The harder the conflict, the more glorious the triumph. What we obtain too cheap, we esteem too lightly; it is dearness only that gives everything value. I love the one who can smile in trouble, who can gather strength from distress and grow brave by reflection.

Thomas Paine, adapted

Character cannot be developed in ease and quiet. Only through experience of trial and suffering can the soul be strengthened, ambition inspired, and success achieved.

Helen Keller

You gain strength, courage and confidence by every experience in which you really stop to look fear in the face. You are able to say to yourself, "I have lived through this horror. I can take the next thing that comes along." You must do the thing you think you cannot do.

Eleanor Roosevelt

The most valuable piece of jewelry I own isn't worth much money. It's a small ring: a brown stone with a yellow center mounted in a plain silver setting. Some people call this stone a tiger's eye. I have also heard it referred to as a cat's eye.

When our oldest son, Nick, was almost eight years old, a mysterious lump appeared on his back. The doctor didn't think it was anything to be concerned about but wanted to remove it. When I heard the word *surgery*, all sorts of possibilities ran through my mind. What if it was cancer? What if something went wrong with the anesthesia and my son never woke up? (I have a very active imagination—at times it can rage as out of control as my hormones.)

Nick has asthma and when he was younger he was in and out of the hospital frequently. He became highly suspicious of anyone in a white lab coat who came at him smiling and saying, "this won't hurt but a minute." So, when the doctor told Nick not to worry because this procedure was no big deal, Nick didn't buy it.

The night before he was to have surgery, my mother slid the tiger's eye ring on Nick's finger. "This is a courage ring," she said. "Every time you look at it, remember that God loves you. He's watching over you and that will make you brave."

Nick's surgery went well. But a few months later, *Mama* was diagnosed with terminal cancer. On one particularly bad day, Nick and I gave her the courage ring back. Without saying a word, she slipped it on her finger. I have never seen anyone face death with as much strength and dignity as she did, but I also know the source of her courage—and it wasn't the ring.

From time to time I get that ring out of my jewelry box. I wear it as a reminder of Mama's love, and of her example of what faith can do.

One of my favorite books is *The Hiding Place*, the true story of Corrie ten Boom's life. Corrie lived with her parents and sister in Holland during World War II. They were devout Christians who risked their lives to hide Jews from the Nazis.

As a young child, Corrie idolized her father, and like most children, she asked a lot of questions. One day a neighbor's baby died. When Corrie saw the young infant, she reached out to touch its soft cheek. The baby's skin was cold to her touch and Corrie withdrew, frightened. Later, while on a train, she asked her father about the baby and about death. His answer comforted her—and it has comforted me too during many difficult times.

Corrie's father compared death to getting on a train. He asked young Corrie if she remembered at what point the conductor had given her the ticket. She replied, "Why, just before we got on the train."

"Exactly. And our wise Father in heaven knows when we're going to need things, too. Don't run out ahead of Him, Corrie. When the time comes that some of us will have to die, you will look into your heart and find the strength you need—just in time."

Mama found the strength to get through her illness and ultimately to face death. Corrie relied on her faith to keep her strong when her father died and again when she and her sister faced the horrors of life at a concentration camp. This is what Mama and Corrie both knew: No matter what problems we face—large or small, trivial or significant—God cares for us and will be with us always, even to the end, if we trust in him.

Faith is central. It doesn't always relieve the strains of life, but it gives us a place to seek comfort, a safe haven from life's storms. When the weight of stress bears down on our shoulders, we can respond with prayers for guidance. God didn't promise our journeys would be stress-free, but he promised to be there for us: "Let God train you, for he is doing what any loving father does for his children. Whoever heard of a son who was never corrected?" (Hebrews 12:7).

In *Near to the Heart of God: Daily Readings from the Spiritual Classics,* William Tyndale's words about faith are recorded:

If God sends you to sea, promising to go with you and bring you back safely to land, he will bring a storm against you. He wants you to feel your faith and see his goodness. If it were always fair weather and you were never at risk, your faith would be a mere presumption. You would be unthankful to God and merciless toward your neighbor. . . .

Tribulation is a blessing according to Christ. "Blessed are those who are persecuted because of righteousness, for theirs is the kingdom of heaven" (Matthew 5:10, NIV).

Often in our faith journeys, God guides us to seek those who are gifted in helping us through our pain, perhaps through a friend or through trained professionals—counselors, doctors, therapists—who help us discover solutions that we didn't previously see. Some of us don't want to seek professional help (even though we feel we need it) because we are ashamed or afraid to reach out. But there are many professionals who are competent and caring and have dedicated their lives to helping others. A small step toward their help can sometimes make a big difference in our lives.

According to the *Mayo Clinic Guide to Self-Care,* "When we respond to stress with anxiety, tension or worry, that response is not just 'mental.' When we feel threatened in some way, chemical 'messengers' are released, producing physical changes such as rapid pulse, quick breathing and dry mouth. These changes prepare the body for 'fight or flight.' If we react to stress for long periods, it may contribute to physical or emotional illness."

When that happens, there are signs and symptoms that may serve as a warning. If any of these symptoms consistently apply to you, see a doctor or seek appropriate professional help. Here are some of the signs and symptoms of stress that *Guide to Self-Care* says to be aware of:

Physical	
Headaches	Muscle aches
Grinding teeth	Indigestion
Tight, dry throat	Constipation/diarrhea
Clenched jaws	Increased perspiration
Chest pain	Cold, sweaty hands
Shortness of breath	Fatigue
Pounding heart	Insomnia
High blood pressure	Frequent illness

Psychological	
Anxiety	Feeling of worthlessness
Irritability	Feeling of lack of direction
Feeling of impending danger or doom	Feeling of insecurity
Depression	Sadness
Slowed thinking	Defensiveness
Racing thoughts	Anger
Feeling of helplessness	Hypersensitivity
Feeling of hopelessness	Apathy

Behavioral	
Overeating/loss of appetite	Avoiding or neglecting responsibility
Impatience	Poor job performance
Argumentativeness	Burnout
Procrastination	Poor personal hygiene
Increased use of alcohol or drugs	Change in religious practices
Increased smoking	Change in family or close relationships
Withdrawal or isolation	

You are a VIW (Very Important Woman); treat yourself accordingly. If you find that these symptoms keep popping up, take care of yourself. *Be-*

lieve that God cares for you. *Believe* that Jesus, while he was on earth, experienced tremendous stress. He understands how you feel. *Trust* him to help you find the solutions to your problems. *Have faith* that there is competent help available—professional and pastoral—to get you through especially difficult times.

In John Jesus says, "Do not let your hearts be troubled. Trust in God, trust also in me" (14:1, NIV). Remember, no problem you have is too big for God.

DEstressors

Identifying Your Stress Points and Developing a Plan of Action

1. Do you feel spiritually weak when the stress points come? Here are some suggestions for a spiritual workout to help you gain strength:

   • Spend a short time every day reading the Bible.
   • To find rest and restoration, read a psalm a day.
   • To discover how to take on your stress factors, study the Gospels. Observe the various ways that Jesus faced stress.
   • Once you've discovered some of the ways Jesus handled stress, you have a model to work from. Based on this model, design a plan for dealing with your top three stressors. Next week, take on the three next stressors.

2. If you have been under stress for a long period of time and that stress affects you mentally and physically, how are you coping? If you are merely surviving, then here are a few things you

can do to gain strength in these stressful times:

- *Discuss your problems* with your spouse, your minister, and/or a close friend. Get their input. Perhaps they can offer you practical solutions for your stress—or maybe just talking about your burdens will help you discover a solution.
- *Ask for prayer.* One—or all—of these people will probably be willing to pray for you about these burdens. Ask them to. If you feel comfortable doing so, you can ask them to pray *with* you.
- *Get professional help.* Especially if the signs of stress seem physical, go to a medical doctor for a complete examination. If your burdens still continue to feel too heavy, consider seeking professional counseling. If you don't feel secure about seeking counseling, talk to someone you respect who has benefited from counseling and can recommend a good resource.

Mary Alice's Story

God Knows My Needs

Having been a secondary school teacher for more than thirty years, my life as wife and mother had always operated on the rhythmic cycles of the school year. My children and I were free at the same times—and I truly loved my job: the school I worked for, the students, and my fellow teachers. To say that I was content is a huge understatement. While my colleagues and I often lamented the long hours we were putting in on after-school projects and on the staff development that came as a result of a statewide educational improvement plan, I inwardly relished the feeling of being a part of an exciting new effort.

But a unique set of circumstances brought this part of my life to an abrupt halt. Over a period of years, a troubling situation had developed in the management of our school system that threatened its *entire* program. My nephew was chosen to be candidate for a seat on the school board. If he were to be elected, a shift in the dynamics of the board could begin to make positive changes in this difficult situation. I strongly encouraged him to enter the race, knowing that if he were to be successful, I, as his aunt, would have to resign because of Kentucky's nepotism law. He was elected by a large majority in November, so I had until December 31 to retire. I had seriously planned to retire at the end of the school year, but leaving so abruptly in the middle of a term was more than a little traumatic.

I spent the last days at school trying to keep a positive attitude, but most nights were spent in tears of frustration and anger at a situation that appeared to be grossly unfair. (Three nearby school systems had the same situation but worked to gain permission for the employees to complete the current school year.) I fell into the trap of thinking, "Why me?" My first months of retirement brought little comfort and I felt myself becoming more and more bitter and dissatisfied.

My thinking was yanked back into perspective by a near-fatal car accident one warm spring evening. When I regained consciousness, I was trapped in the overturned vehicle, hanging by the seat belt. My clarity of thought at that moment was amazing; I realized what I had done, and worried that my husband would be upset that I had ruined his truck. And I realized that I very well might be dying. Strangely, there was no sense of panic or fear—I felt completely safe and secure in the feeling that God was there with me. I was able to give thanks for the life I had, and to simply ask that he would be with me in whatever was to come.

And he was—through the Stat-Flight, through resuscitation and life support techniques, through many hours of surgery to rebuild the bone structure of my face, and through a painful and agonizingly slow recovery. My family was incredibly supportive, and friends and former students and teaching colleagues helped keep my spirit up throughout.

At the end of the ordeal, almost back to my normal self physically, my contentment and feeling of being at peace with my life situation allowed me to rejoice with each day's appearance. I no longer looked backward but instead turned to new efforts. When strength allowed, I once again enjoyed my yard and garden work, and the tennis that gives me so much pleasure. I went back to graduate school (now that was a scary moment after twenty years as a nonstudent!) for two classes to prepare for a position as adjunct professor in our local university.

My schedule now allows long weekend visits with my children and their families and time for travel with my husband, sisters, and friends.

I am so thankful that God knows our hearts and our needs better than we do, and time that sometimes things that appear as trials can actually be our greatest blessings.

Mary Alice
(college teacher, wife, mother, grandmother)

Kim's Story

Is It Stress or Is It Something More?

I have a family history of depression; both my mother and grandmother have had serious problems with it. My problem started when I was a teenager, but I didn't get help until something happened to someone I loved. It was very traumatic. I want to share my story with other women because I want them to know that no matter how bad things seem, there is a way to make it through.

Shortly after my daughter's birth I fell into a deep depression that wouldn't go away. I wanted to just disappear and never be heard from again. Talking with my husband helped but it could not make the depression go away, so I went back to see my counselor.

He told me that my depression was severe enough that I needed to take medication, so I stopped nursing and started taking Prozac. My husband noticed the difference first and within a few weeks I felt much better.

When my husband and I decided we wanted to have another baby, I was worried about the depression coming back again. Many women take Prozac while pregnant and nursing and it is not believed to affect the baby. However, I did not want to be dependent on the drug for the rest of my life, so I stopped taking it and did well for several months. Then when I was eight weeks pregnant, I had a miscarriage. When the hormones kicked in, I started crying and couldn't stop. I went for a physical and learned that I had sleep apnea. After I had surgery to correct the apnea I began to sleep better and this made a big difference. After our second child was born, I was very worried about becoming depressed again, but thankfully it didn't happen.

Now I know that there is a difference between stress and depression and I make sure that I do not cross that line. I still go see my counselor every now and then. I also know that if the depression becomes unmanageable, I have the option of medication. Because of my family history, I realize that there is probably a chemical imbalance in my brain that causes the depression and medication helps with that.

A little stress is okay, as long as I keep it from becoming depression, and I have learned that there are things I can do to combat stress. First, I always try to keep in mind that it could be worse. Many things have gone wrong this year for my family but none of them was life threatening and we have overcome them without major trauma. Also, I try not to miss an opportunity to fellowship with other Christian women. This association lets you know you are not alone and that the same things that stress you, stress other women, too. At our congregation we have a monthly ladies' night out and I really look forward to spending time with my friends. I don't miss the ladies' retreat, no matter how much trouble it is to get the husband and kids situated for twenty-four hours while I'm away.

I don't want my daughter to have the self-esteem problems that I had as a child, and I know the amount of stress I can manage is directly affected by how I feel about myself, so I work hard at maintaining a healthy level of self-esteem. It makes me feel good when someone thanks me for something I have done, and I return the favor by making a special effort to thank others for the blessings they give me and to congratulate them for their accomplishments.

If the depression comes back, I know now that I can control it. I would not hesitate to go back on Prozac or some other drug if that is what it takes to keep balance in my life. I also have the love and support of my family and my church family to see me through.

Kim (wife, mother, and videographer)

What Other Women Have to Say

Comments on Breaking the Stress Barrier

I don't usually deal with stress until it gets the best of me. I have trouble saying no, and I go and go until I'm worn out physically and emotionally. Then I have a good cry and go to bed. A lot of my stress is over trying to "fix" things that I can't. During my hardest times, I have been able to turn my worries over to the Lord. It seems the little stuff that I try to handle myself is what causes me the most problems.

Martha (teacher, wife, and mother of three)

I find when I'm under stress, a quiet time of prayer and Bible reading of special verses or passages tends to put my mind and body at rest. Reviewing these special verses brings me to a place of trust in the One who gives peace. He will not let me be tempted or tried above that which I can handle. Every trial has a purpose: My bout with cancer has brought me closer to God and my family.

Jeanette (age 63, retired)

My biggest stress is that I want to feel needed and

useful and that I want my activities to be productive and of value. I also worry that my children will have to take care of me.

Martha (retired teacher)

A Final Thought about Stress and Perception

While writing *The Knot at the End of Your Rope*, I found one of my old journals. I opened it up and found an entry just right for a concluding piece.

So much of this book has been about our approach and our attitudes toward stress. The following entry in my journal reminds me that the *amount* of stress I feel is directly connected to my *perception* of the problem. The next time you feel stressed, examine your perception of the stressors and remember that *you can do something* about the stress level and your attitude. Try one or more of the strategies suggested in this book. Other women have used them successfully. My hope and prayer is that they will help you too.

December 1993

God, today I am knee deep in dirty laundry. A pan got stuck in the dishwasher this morning, and when I yanked . . . nothing happened, so I had a fight with the dishwasher and it won. I lost my temper (forgive me, Lord) and the madder I got, the harder I pulled. When the whole machine came out of the wall and I landed on my backside, I threw in the white dishtowel.

On top of that, the refrigerator died. The repairman came and told me I might as well bury it. While I was cleaning it out, a ketchup bottle fell on the floor and exploded. My son heard me scream, saw the red liquid splattered on the cabinets and walls, thought I was mortally wounded and promptly dialed 911.

The weatherman is predicting snow and ice for the next week, which means no school and a house full of kids going in and out, tracking snow and slush and making more dirty laundry. God, if another appliance has to die, please don't let it be the washer or dryer.

And I wonder, what did I do to deserve all this?

But then night falls, and even though I'm exhausted, I read five bedtime stories and tuck five beautiful children into bed. I listen to five sets of prayers that all end by asking God to "bless Mommy and Daddy." I breathe in the sweet perfume of shampoo and baby powder and feel the soft touch of wet kisses on my cheek.

And I can't help but wonder, dear God, what could I possibly have done to deserve all of this?